OPTIONS TRADING FOR BEGINNERS

Learn all the Strategies and The Basics of Investing in The Stock Market to Make Profit for And Living with Trading Options

BY

Ray Lantrip

Disclaimer Notice:

Please note the information contained within this document is for educational and entertainment purposes only. All effort has been executed to present accurate, up-to-date, and reliable, complete information. No warranties of any kind are declared or implied. Readers acknowledge that the author is not engaging in the rendering of legal, financial, medical, or professional advice. The content within this book has been derived from various sources. Please consult a licensed professional before attempting any techniques outlined in this book.

By reading this document, the reader agrees that under no circumstances is the author responsible for any losses, direct or indirect, which are incurred as a result of the use of the information contained within this document, including, but not limited to, — errors, omissions, or inaccuracies.

Table of Contents

INTRODUCTION

It is very boring to have a routine every day. Tying oneself to jobs that require tons of paperwork is dull and uninteresting for most workers. On the contrary, some individuals like options trading, get to do high-paying jobs.

There are arguably a relatively good number of reasons behind the trading of options. For one thing, in smaller periods, this specific venture boasts high-earning investments. It is undoubtedly a great way to boost your monthly income and support all of your financial needs and desires. How to make money with options, on the other hand, requires patience and time. With the terminology and basics of the world of options, you must continuously learn and educate yourself. So how can you begin your career in trading options?

Know the difference between investments that are long-term and short-term. You've got something to put your money on that works. The benefits involved in trading options could be enormous, and it is an excellent way to start your venture to know where to invest and how to extend its benefits.

Determine the sort of options that work best for you. If you can make cash with options, whether it is a call or a put, you have to assess easily. Due to a lack of evaluation, trading techniques often fail. In determining whether you should invest or purchase a put or call option, timing is also a key element. What matters is that you know which type is most advantageous for you.

With options trading, learning how to make cash always starts with research. You have to maximize every chance and try to know what is necessary for that company. You can always begin by participating in trading or buying specific stocks. As time progresses, depending on your acquired experience and previous trading performance, you can eventually decide on being a writer or bookie. And while these tips help you start a career in the trading of options, you can now understand that greener pastures are everywhere. You can learn the techniques and techniques provided in the book, and you can know more about how to achieve success in the trading of options. Trading options is a passive revenue-generating program that you will benefit from and live the beautiful and prosperous life you desire so much.

CHAPTER ONE

VARIETY OF TRADING OPTIONS

Like traditional market trading, binary options trading provides investors with many options to execute their investment strategy. Investments based on brief-term projections are binary options. Like traditional trading, by researching in advance and through the knowledge they gain while gaining trading experience, investors can learn options trading.

There are several reasons for learning trading options. Still, these often return to four key elements: trading is simplistic, provides investors with the opportunity for significant profits, results in rapid returns, and enables investors to trade across a wide range of assets. For these four reasons alone, it makes sense to spend time and effort learning about trading options.

Its simplicity is at the very core of digital options. Options across a range of platforms offer an easy-to-learn process. Most binary options platforms, including past trading, provide ample information on the different assets available. Investors need to decide whether an investment will increase (by executing a CALL option) or fall in price (by completing a PUT option). Once it is selected and a bid is placed, investors have to wait to see whether their trade has been successful.

They give themselves the chance to experience high-profit potential when an investor takes the time to learn options trading. Because options operate on short-term projections, investors can place bids throughout the day and receive multiple payouts across various categories of assets. The probability of greater profits is available for the taking as knowledge and experience are acquired.

Because binary options operate on fast turnaround times, quick returns also mean fast returns. Most binary options expire in less than one hour, some expire in a few hours, so this offers the opportunity throughout the trading day to experience returns over and over again.

Finally, but certainly not least, is the range of assets traded with binary options by an investor. This fact, in itself, makes it worthwhile to learn about trading binary options. Trades in various asset categories will be offered by most platforms, including stocks, indices, currency pairs, and commodities such as crude oil, natural gas, gold, and silver. This asset portfolio enables investors to diversify their portfolio for the greatest return on their investment.

The magic of trading options is that it makes it possible to match different stock trading philosophies with various strategies. Each strategy has an additional profitability and risk tolerance level and can spice up a portfolio very nicely using multiple techniques! I will outline four distinct stock trading strategies in this section and how they can be matched with corresponding trading strategies for options that you can apply to your portfolio. The main idea is to first concentrate on an underlying stock trading strategy and then, by using options, add significant leverage and power to the trade.

The concept of TIME DECAY is the most critical factor when considering each of these strategies. The value of any option decreases over time until the day the option expires. This idea can be the primary enemy of any trade-in options, eating into their profits, or it can be the key to successful and profitable trading of options.

Firstly, which approach?

There are usually four different strategies employed by stock traders, each of which, when applied to options, has consequences:

(i) Position Trading

Traders buy a stock and hold it, based on its excellent fundamentals, for long periods. To reach excellent value, they will often wait for a stock and then watch for institutional or insider buying before making a move. They look out for other buyers to step in and move the price even further as the stock price increases.

It is NOT appropriate to buy calls and puts because you pay large premiums for the time value, most of which could be wiped out over time even as the stock gains. Your enemy is TIME DECAY.

In the option cycle on the stock you already own, selling covered calls every month can reduce the cost you paid for the stock in the first trade significantly. You can still be a winner even if the stock goes down!

(ii) Momentum or Trend trading

Once a stock has made a clear move or breakout, Momentum's traders step in and ride the stock up to its first significant reversal along with a trend. They hope to make shorter-term profits for periods of holding range from six weeks to six months from a rapid move in the price.

It is NOT appropriate to purchase calls and puts because you pay large premiums for time value, most of which will be wiped out over time even as the stock gains. With Momentum Trading, TIME DECAY is your enemy unless you have a powerful and fast-moving trend.

Selling credit spreads is the right approach and can be very profitable because as you sell spreads from the direction of the stock's momentum on the opposite leg (e.g., selling put credit spreads in stock with a strong bullish trend). You can buy back the spreads repeatedly at minimum cost and sell another spread closer in. This approach can easily yield 10-15 percent per month of profit. Your secret weapon for trading this approach is Time Decay.

It is a good strategy to sell Naked Puts and can be even more profitable than selling credit spreads. However, it leaves you a position that if the trade goes against you, you might have to buy a lot of stock, so your broker requires you to have a lot of margins.

(iii) Swing Trading

Swing Traders within a trend, buy and sell swings or oscillations. The holding time ranges from 2 to 10 days. This way is a shorter-term trading technique that depends more on the trend's direction than on fundamental indicators or technical indicators.

You will be able to start buying calls and puts, or DITM options, which will take you to real profits if you have mastered the ability to identify reversals or swings within a trend and know how to plan an exit strategy! Holding times are short (2-10 days) with Swing Trading, and so you minimize the effect of TIME DECAY, your arch enemy.

(iv) Day Trading

The many small moves during the trading day, mainly shown by candlestick patterns, are focused on day traders. This approach has a broker's requirement to qualify for a minimum of $25,000, which knocks out many beginners.

With this strategy, option trading is not suitable. Broker fees are relatively high for trading options, and day traders end up paying their brokers vast amounts. If you own a stock of at least 100 units that are not mainly trending in any specific direction, sell Covered Calls in the option cycle every month. The net price you originally paid for the stock can be reduced by between 5-12 percent each month.

You can easily sell Credit Spreads or Sell Naked Puts every month in the option cycle if you have at least $1,000 in your account and can identify a trend. You can start buying Calls and Puts, or DITM options, and make phenomenal profits if you have mastered Swing Trading principles, especially the idea of planning entries and exits.

Many concepts are often misunderstood in the world of options trading. Terms such as put option, option to call, weekly options, contract with derivatives, spread trade, and the list go on and on.

The stock options contract is one of the more common concepts that is misunderstood.

What Exactly Is a Stock Options Contract?

While it may seem confusing at first sight, it is far easier than it is made out to be.

Let's start with a basic definition of an option; an option gives the buyer the right but not the duty to buy or sell the underlying option at a certain price in the future by a specific date.

Precisely that is what an option is - the ability to be long or short of the underlying price at a certain price by a specific date in the future. This contract type is always based on an underlying agreement or shares.

In the case of an inventory, one contract is equal to 100 shares of the inventory. In the future, one contract is similar to the underlying end.

Called strike prices, options have set price levels.

Options always involve a special price that is known as the strike or striking price. This strike price is when the underlying contract can be bought or sold at which one may have the right.

Often referred to as the exercise price, the strike price is. There will be more strike prices for some underlying contracts than others. For example, inexpensive stocks may have $2.50 strike price increases, while more moderately priced stocks may have $5.00, with even larger gains in costly stocks.

Let's take an example: Let's assume an investor is trading XYZ shares that are currently trading at $25 per share.

Furthermore, let's assume that this investor believes that the shares may rise soon but does not want to commit the capital necessary to buy the shares directly.

Instead, the investor may elect to buy a call option. The investor may elect to purchase a $27.50 call for the first month in this specific case. This call contract would give the investor the right to buy the shares, or the shares would be long from $27.50 at any time until expiration, but not the obligation.

Let's assume that the shares skyrocket to $30 per share after the investor buys this call contract. If the investor has an obligation to be $27.50 long, the investor will look at a $2.50 per share gain on the shares minus whatever premium they paid for the call.

While we will address call options and put options more specifically in a future section, one must have a thorough understanding of how these contracts work before looking to use them.

Options Always have a date of expiration.

It will always have an expiration date when an option is listed.

These days, there are many different expiration dates, and more will probably be introduced in the future. Other inventories and various goods may also have different expiration dates.

Most heavily traded stocks, for example, will have options that expire each month. These options expire each month on the third Friday of the month. Also, some stocks will have listed end-of-month options as well as listed weekly options.

The point is that a finite lifespan has every option.

Since options have a finite lifespan, an option will experience time decay, otherwise known as theta decay, all else remaining equal during its life. Theta is one of the most well-known Greek options and must be well understood to take advantage of alternatives.

Why do options have a date of expiration? Well, a leveraged transfer of risk is one way of looking at an option contract.

The idea of an option contract is the same as an insurance policy in many respects.

There is always a period attached to it when one purchases an insurance policy. Each year, many policies must be renewed. You pay the insurance company a premium during the policy term to assume the risk of loss during that period. The insurance company will no longer take that risk once the term expires unless the policy is renewed and another premium is paid.

Options are very similar in that an option seller assumes the risk of a particular move being made by a stock or underlying contract. A premium is paid to the option vendor, like the insurance company. However, once that option expires, the risk is no longer assumed by the option seller.

Options Can Be In, Out, or At-The-Money

A contract can be in-the-money, out-of-the-money, or at-the-money when looking at option contracts.

An in-the-money option is a contract option whose strike price is greater than or less than the current underlying price. For example, if JJJ shares are trading at $50 per share and one owns the $45 call, because the shares are already trading above the strike price, that call option would be considered in-the-money.

If one owns the $50 call option, using the same example, that option would be considered at-the-money because it is at the level at which the underlying shares are currently trading.

Finally, because the underlying shares are not at or above the strike price of $55, the $55 call option would be deemed out-of-the-money.

An Option's Value Is Known as The Premium

The value of an option is known as the premium when options are traded. This premium is the price at which the option can be bought or sold.

In other words, when a speculator wants to purchase the right but not the duty to buy or sell a stock at a specific price in the future by a certain date, he or she will pay a premium to the option seller. If the option expires, then the seller retains the bonus.

Option premiums can have bid/ask spreads that are reasonably narrow or relatively broad. These are often quoted by market makers whose job in that particular option is to make a market.

Market makers are looking to take advantage of the ability to buy the bid and seal the offer. However, the investing public does not have this ability and is likely to buy the offer or sell the bid or perhaps transact somewhere between these levels when trading options.

Option agreements trading for smaller premiums such as less than $3.00 will often trade in increments of $.05, while options trading for larger tips will trade in increments of $.10.

There Are Two Types of Option Value

Two types of value that are known as intrinsic and extrinsic are option contracts.

Intrinsic value is the value of the option derived from being in-the-money, whereas extrinsic value is derived from the option's time value.

Options may consist of both value types at the same time or maybe made up entirely of one or the other.

For instance, an out-of-the-money option will consist entirely of extrinsic or time value, while an almost entirely intrinsic value will consist of a deep-in-the-money option.

There Are Many Option Based Strategies Available

Contracts for options may be bought, sold, or bought and sold in different combinations.

There are two types of contracts for options referred to as a call option and a put option.

A variety of option strategies can be developed and used using these two different types of contracts to hedge existing positions, make a directional bet on a stock or market, or take advantage of the passage of time in attempting to profit from the decay of time.

Trading binary options, or as they are sometimes referred to, digital options, gives traders much more flexibility and options than conventional forms of trading options. This type of trading makes it possible for traders to trade a wide range of financial instruments, including stocks, commodities, currencies, and more. Trading digital options give traders the opportunity in a brief period to realize profits of 60-80% on trades, even as little as one hour in many instances.

The benefits of this trading style are that trading is a simple process, and as opposed to conventional trading options, there is limited risk involved. To profit, traders only have to be correct as far as price direction is concerned. Twenty-four hours a day, binary options are issued, and the trader can select different time frames for each trade. The risk involved is fixed and predetermined, so traders exactly know what the profit or loss on any given business will be.

Digital options are less risky than other trading forms, mainly Forex because there are no leverage conditions or 'stop-loss' involved. Traders do not have to worry about trades going against their position and incurring enormous losses. In each transaction, the risk is always limited to the amount invested. This manner gives traders the flexibility to trade with only a small amount of risk, even in the most volatile markets.

Profits are realized by a single tick as trades go into the money. To realize profits, traders don't have to worry about the price reaching a certain point.

With binary options trading, traders never need to worry about margin calls. The minimum account required to start trading is much less than what is necessary for other markets, such as Forex, commodities, and stocks, to trade.

On what can be traded, there is virtually no limit. The most popular instruments, such as currencies, gold, oil, and stocks, are issued with options.

Other advantages include:

- Trading can be diversified easily
- Alternatives expire hourly and daily
- Options on the secondary market are not traded

Your success must find a good broker. All brokers do not offer the same benefits. Before choosing a broker, check out several brokers and compare the features. When an option expires out of the money, the best brokers will have an out of the money feature that pays up to 15 percent.

A primary benefit of binary options is higher returns. Traders can profit on a single trade by as much as 80 percent.

The speedy returns that are possible are another advantage. In as little as one hour, traders can realize significant returns.

Trading in binary options is becoming more popular because of the unique benefits not found in other trading forms. Traders discover that it is simpler and virtually stress-free to trade binary options, two significant advantages in the investment world.

CHAPTER TWO

OPTION TRADING STRATEGIES FOR BEGINNERS

Options trading has a lot of revenue potential in the stock market world, and if you pick and follow the right strategy, it is full of monetary benefits. There are many strategies for option trading that an investor can choose from. You can select an option strategy, depending on the impression you have about the stock price movement's direction.

Several strategies are mostly used for trading options, such as bullish, bearish, and neutral strategies. Then bullish or bearish strategies are used if you have an impression of the stock price going either way. If you have no clue about the movement of stock prices, then the correct strategy to select is neutral.

If you expect the underlying stock price to rise, then you should use a bullish strategy. With this approach, however, it is essential to examine how the stock price can increase and the period in which the rally will take place. This examination will assist the trader in choosing the best strategy for trading. The call buying strategy, the bull put spread, bull call spread, short put approach, the long call, the covered call, the protective put, and the collar strategy are some of the most common bullish option trading strategies used in the stock market. The call buying strategy is the most bullish, whereas the bull's spread and the moderate are the bull call spreads. You will make money with this strategy as long as the stock price does not drop by the expiry date.

If you speculate that there will be a downward trend in the underlying stock price, the bearish options trading strategy is the right one to pick, which is the opposite of the bullish strategy. In the case of a bearish scenario, to select the best trading strategy, it is necessary to understand the level and the time frame at which a stock's prices will fall. Short call, long put, short synthetic, put back spread, call bear spread, and put bear spread is generally executed bearish strategies. The most bearish trading strategy of all options is the put buying strategy, which is mostly practiced in this field by beginners. The call bear spread and the put bear spread are the strategies of moderately bearish options.

You should choose a neutral options trading strategy, which is also known as a non-directional trading strategy if you are clueless about the underlying stock price movement. The potential profit is dependent on the volatility of the stock price underlying it. Straddle and Butterfly are some famous examples of neutral trading strategies.

You'd buy or sell option derivatives in the Straddle strategy. If the trader purchases the derivative, it is known as a long straddle, whereas it is known as a short straddle when the trader sells the product. A less risky trading strategy for options is the Butterfly strategy. Two positions, the long butterfly position and the short butterfly position, are included in this strategy. If the future volatility is lower than the implied volatility, then in a long butterfly, you would make a profit. Simultaneously, in a short butterfly, you only make a profit when the future volatility of the underlying stock is higher than the stock's implied volatility.

There are other commonly used strategies, such as strangle, guts, risk reversal, and condor, in addition to these two neutral strategies.

As they have heard stories making promises of fast profits, many opportunity seekers are attracted to options trading. The problem is that in a short period, these traders come to think of nothing but stuffing their bank accounts full of cash. While this scenario is achievable, the odds against you are certainly going well. In most cases, achieving large profits in a short period involves a trading strategy of extremely high-risk options. Finding a dependable approach and mastering it is the key to your success. Rather than hitting a home run, it is far better to pull off consistent gains. Once you know one approach, you can learn other ones well.

Below are some of the trading strategies for options that you might consider.

Selling Credit Spreads - If you are looking for a strategy that doesn't involve marrying your career with stock options, then you might consider this one. There is nothing worse for every minute of the trading day than following a strategy that requires you to monitor the market. In about an hour a week, you can complete what is involved with this strategy, and if done correctly, you could increase your portfolio by around 10-15 percent monthly. These are great returns that put what the banks offer to shame. You need to know how to conduct trend analysis on the market to execute this approach. The scope of this section, of course, does not allow me to cover it further. On this site, you are best advised to join the mailing list.

Bullish Strategy - If you expect to increase an option's underlying stock, you could go with this approach. When the trader expects the underlying stock price to rise in value, the Bullish options trading strategies are brought into play. You need to consider just how high it is likely that the stock price will go and within what time frame. A simple call buying strategy is the most likely choice of method for a bullish trader. With beginners, this is quite popular. Covered Straddle, Bull Calendar Spread, and The Collar are other bullish strategies.

Complex strategies - These include things like iron condors, butterflies, straddles, and strangles. Just where do they come up with the names used in option trading strategies? Odd, aren't they? If correctly followed, the ones I have listed here are generally low risk while being highly likely to be profitable at the same time. The downside is that they are costly, either because you are trading expensive options or because of high brokerage fees because of the number of trades involved.

It would help if you remembered that options are relatively flexible tools for trading. This fact is where many people get it right with such great flexibility. They believe that the more complex the trading strategy for an option is, the more successful it can be. It can be quite the opposite. The more complex the procedure, the more open you can be to risk while limiting the potential for profit at the same time.

As with any strategy, you use and treat your options trading company with respect. Until you have given it a good test utilizing a practice account, do not trade live. Only then should you consider using your real money to run with it.

It is always advisable to only use risk capital when trading with real cash when learning how to trade options. This fact implies that if you have trades that go against you, you can only use the money you can afford to lose. There you go, just touching the surface of trading strategies for options. Of course, you'll want to learn more and then choose a method that uses a test account to trade your options. Who knows from over there?

Please always remember not to let things get out of hand. If you are learning a new approach, trade with only one agreement at a time. You will soon find yourself out of control and headed towards disaster if you go overboard. Trading in options is not a race. You've got time on your side, and you should contact the most out of it. Tomorrow the market will still be here.

Best Day Option Trading Strategies

For traders, having a well-crafted binary options trading strategy is an asset. It will enable them to overcome any unexpected financial market events. The binary options sector is very volatile, so it isn't easy to have a unique strategy to suit all circumstances.

However, the trader can follow specific rules that guide him throughout his trading trip, maximizing his returns.

Monitoring the Financial Market

Financial market monitoring is an essential strategy that each trader should adopt when talking about online trading. It is also a primary element of a successful trade to record the trends the assets are following. The two devices that can be used to keep an eye on the directions in which the assets move are:

Technical Analysis - Technical analysis is an instrument that analyzes past trends in financial prices to forecast future trends. It is a very effective method since it analyzes the demand and supply related to a particular market. Therefore, the technical analysis can determine the direction the market will continue to follow in the future from the data obtained. The data generated by this analysis can alter the traders' game.

Statistical analysis - Also, statistical analysis is available. At first glance, it may seem not very easy, as not every trader has a statistical concept. However, the trader does not need to embark on complex calculations as, fortunately, some brokerage companies offer a service known as the Daily Market Analysis. These are daily reports issued by experts carrying out an in-depth analysis of the entire market. In general, the reports cover the overall performance of assets such as inventories, indices, currencies, and commodities.

Traders should not neglect the importance of monitoring the market as it is the key to maximizing their profitable trades.

Choose a Trading Tool and Practice

One common approach that traders can use is known as Day Trading. This type of trade is referred to as a trade involving the purchase and sale, within 24 hours, of stocks. It is highly recommended because traders can generate a large volume of returns using this strategy only by tracking small price movements. Here are some tips to be successful with day-trading:

Set an Entry Price - It is recommended that traders set an entry price to avoid being too emotional during the trade. It may happen that during a transaction, gluttony takes over, which is the trader decides to invest much more than he initially planned. As the latter's judgment is affected by his feelings, this behavior can be dangerous. This kind of behavior can lead to a loss for the trader. Therefore, to ensure that the trader's psychological frame will not interfere in his trades, it is crucial to set an entry price.

Follow the trend intra-day - The trader should follow the trend intra-day. That is, by following the trend, traders will significantly reduce risk when they trade. Although the intra-day trend will reverse simultaneously, it still allows the traders to generate high profits.

Keep a record of the trades that have been made - All traders should keep a record of their results. Besides, writing a list of the losing and winning trades, even if it takes time, will help the traders to know exactly what they did right and what they did wrong. This list will act as a personal guideline of the do's and don't of day trade based on their personal experience.

Money Management

It is essential to have a good money management strategy while talking about binary options; otherwise, the trader will find himself at the wrong end of the market. Sometimes losing specific trades is inevitable, so it is even more critical to have a good money management strategy to ensure that the losing trades do not exhaust all the money invested. The traders should aim to end up with a substantial profit that will cover their original investment instead of aiming to win all the trades. A well-conceived strategy will consist of only 5% of the initial capital being invested. If the trader's initial investment is $2000, the trader should not invest more than $100 in each trade.

Obviously, as trading only 5 percent of the capital will generate low returns, it takes a lot of patience. However, the risks of producing enormous losses will be significantly reduced.

Nowadays, online trading is becoming increasingly popular and attracts a vast number of traders annually. To be prepared to face these ruthless traders in the industry, they need a strategy to help them cope with all unexpected contingencies. The essential element that traders should bear in mind is that their best ally is time and patience.

Volatility in the Market

The economy consists of three fundamental sectors: agriculture, manufacturing, and services. The real economy of a society is shaped jointly by those sectors. In regulating all these sectors, the government plays an important role. Moreover, a few severe economic activities, such as defense, currency, and some public goods, are carried out by modern societies' governments. The monetary sector is an essential aspect of all economies. The economic sector does not directly provide any tangible benefit to an individual, but it is inevitable for the product and service sectors to function smoothly. The complete and understandable picture of an economy is represented by the inclusion of monetary or financial instruments. By defining prices, return rates, and exchange rates, the financial sector removes several frictions between individuals/institutions/states. The critical aspect of the financial economy is the stock markets. They provide avenues for companies to collect capital, and investors receive dividends from businesses in return. Speculative activities and deep learning of the economic agents involved are the byproducts of the stock market. Financial markets are now an unavoidable component of any economy. There are five major players in the stock market: speculators, investors, corporations, brokers, and the government. The volatile environment in the market is created by volatility or an uncertain extreme response to an event by all major players. Technically speaking, volatility is a statistical measure of the dispersion of returns for a given security or market index. Volatility can be measured either using the standard deviation or using the variance between returns from that same security or market index. Usually, the higher the volatility, the riskier the security or market.

Bases of Stock Market Volatility

Five major players in the stock market are involved: speculators, investors, brokers, business firms, and government or regulatory bodies. Because of personal emotions such as greed, fear, panic, and dogmatic arrangements, speculators are volatile. Owing to peculiar beliefs about price/volume patterns and companies and governments' decisions, they manifest volatility now and then. Also, speculators want a stable return from the windfall, come what may. Due to a lack of information, knowledge, and understanding, investors show volatility. Naively or wrongly, investors channel trust/expectations to some companies, indices, and regulatory bodies. The volatility of brokers is usually the result of unfair competition between broker firms, broker houses' rent-seeking activity to avoid a few regulations, and trader exploitation. Instead of low input productivity, business firms may show volatility, a top management decision-making framework, and inadequate government regulations. Global economic conditions also have a positive and negative effect on local firms' behavior and their share prices. Because of multiple political appropriateness, government manifests extremity. Significant business players/associations are pressuring governments for specific economic policies.

Beliefs & Market Uncertainty of Investors

A belief is an invisible force against multiple stimuli behind actions or deterrence. Due to knowledge, observation, experience, and contemplation, an idea is formed. It feeds or gives strength to human reason and intuition whenever a belief is established. Logic and intuition, both economic and non-economic, are naturally endowed arms for any life struggle. The Stock Market is also a complex function of thinking and intuitive players in the market. A market player's conflicting reasoning or/and fixed intuitive mindset generates a wave of uncertainty among all financial market participants. Sustained tension implies market chaos. The outcome of confusion, however, is the creation of relatively better and more meaningful beliefs. Due to some rational/intuitive fallacy, there is a possibility of incorrect opinions or conclusions about the financial market's operation. The recurring "Market Correction" phenomenon activates the invincible stock market warriors, Time, and Patience.

Consequently, it follows a reasonable/intuitive belief pattern. It is noteworthy that due to conflicting human nature, the very existence of skewed price/volume movement is a permanent feature of a share market so that a share market is an endless battleground for all. Time-efficiency and patience are always the ultimate winners.

Working & Market Uncertainty by Investors

Investors are essential and vital players in an economy. And they are building blocks for the results of the stock market. So the individual investor is the final basis of all the market's trading activities. They trade with a definite and independent mindset. The market structure develops a strengthening interdependence between investors, and the interdependent investment approach shapes a collective investor mindset. In a few smart individuals, the

34

collective mindset becomes personified. These intelligent people are financial industry leaders. Among some big investors, the maximum benefit accumulation appetite creates uncertainty in the market, now and again. The phenomenon of the bull-bear is a permanent feature of the share market. Efficient-effective market regulators can, to some extent, manage the phenomenon. The proactive role of regulators in creating win-win environments for all and all is inevitable.

Safety Measures

To avoid the aftermath of market volatility, an insightful understanding of shares, a technical and fundamental and proactive response to price/volume movement is essential at the individual level. The long-run solution, however, is the stability of traders, both mental and behavioral. During buying/selling, the impulsive and non-strategic approach badly impacts the traders, particularly at pressures. The intuitive, rational, and strategic position during trading decreases individual traders' effects on buying/selling pressures, which may positively impact market volatility. A comprehensive approach is needed at the collective level to manage multiple volatilities. Government / regulatory bodies can play a preventive as well as a corrective role To harness it. Preventative measures are needed to prevent the stock market's volatility, and disciplinary actions must manage the problems caused by volatility. For disaster management, the respected position of government /

regulatory bodies is essential. Merit killing usually aggravates the situation because of the financial markets' competitive and global nature.

CHAPTER THREE

COMMON BEGINNER MISTAKES

These mistakes were responsible for most of the initial losses that I see making trading options for newbies. Understanding them would certainly help you avoid these mistakes and avoid the initial frustration of losing money.

Mistake 1: Selecting the wrong options (usually out of cash) option

Many trading options for newbies prefer to buy "cheap" from the money options, so buying expensive if cheaper options would also benefit if the stock moved up (for call options). Well, when a stock moved up insignificantly and the role remains in a loss, that one decision alone resulted in much of the initial losses. There are only good out of the money options if you expect the stock to move powerfully in that direction. If you desire to profit from relatively small movements, what you should buy should be in the money or the money options. Many options for trading beginners lose all their money in one go is also to buy out of the cash options. This way occurs when the options they bought never got to expiration in the capital.

Mistake 2: Making complex positions as your first few attempts at trading options

As their first few options trades, many options trading newbies begin making complicated positioning strategies such as iron condor spread or butterfly spreads and then totally screw up as they did not know how to maintain the position. Some do not even know how to set up the parts correctly. If you are new to trading options, stick to making a few simple calls or use a small amount of money (or money you can afford to lose) to use options trades to get a sense of how it works first before moving on to more complicated strategies. Complex strategies are only right when they are as comprehensive as your trading experience.

Mistake 3: Buying options that do not conform to the trading horizon you expect

In the first place, most options trading beginners have no idea what an expected trading horizon is. Generally, they find the alternatives they purchase expiring before the underlying stock made the move they expected it to. Make sure you buy options that are half a year to a year out if you expect a stock to be a mid to long-term performer. If you don't know how a stock will behave, make sure that by buying options with no less than three months to expire, you give yourself plenty of time.

Mistake 4: Placing the wrong orders

Yes, beginners tend to make stupid human errors when under pressure. Especially when real money is involved, such as clicking a wrong button, buying a wrong choice, purchasing a wrong expiration month, or placing a wrong stop-loss order sold off immediately the position. Only through an extended period of virtual trading practice on your chosen options platform can such new human errors. These errors are reduced and then gradually practice using only very little money to get used to the feeling of real money trading. Unfortunately, we are all human; while experienced traders of options tend to make less of such errors, sometimes they still do. Nevertheless, it is more common in newbie trades and hurts trading confidence. Always give yourself a few months of virtual trading practice before going for real money on your chosen platform.

Mistake 5: Trading with money borrowed (or money you cannot afford to lose)

"You can't afford to win if you can't afford to lose," there is a saying. In trading, this is exceptionally true, not only trading options, but any trading. When you trade using cash that you can not afford to lose, when your chances of winning are already very low as a beginner, the mental pressure will reduce your chances of winning. This fact is why we always advise individuals to only trade in money that they can afford to lose.

Mistake 6: Without guidance, trading

Without anybody guiding you, would you learn to drive a car? Why then, without anyone guiding you, would you learn to trade? Yes, for beginners in options trading, a mentor or teacher is extremely important not because they can give you "tips" but because they can shed light on your situation and reveal weaknesses that you may not have noticed. Typically, trading newbies without guidance repeats errors repeatedly, and if you have traded options before, you know it doesn't take many of those errors to wipe out your account.

Pitfalls You Should Avoid

Trading binary options are up-and-coming, but not everyone succeeds in the trade, while others appear to make profits when trading on an ongoing basis. Preparedness is probably the difference between those that follow and those that fail. When you think of getting into the trade, the first thing you should do is learn as much as possible, particularly the basics of binary options. You will be able to avoid the mistakes most traders make when they start this way. Here are a few of the most common errors at all possible costs that you should avoid.

Not creating a trading strategy and using it.

As a new trader, the worst mistake you can make is to invest based solely on how you feel about a given asset or on the advice you got from the TV or other traders. This fact is just random trading, and it's not going to do you any good. Always have a trading strategy in place to avoid losing your money. It should define trading assets, the type of binary option to use, the time frame, and the instruments you will use to generate the trading signals to guide you through. A strategy makes trade more systematic and organized, ultimately maximizing the outcomes.

Poor management of money

It is among the leading causes of failure in the trading of binary options. Most traders spend their time analyzing assets, searching for new trade indicators, and experimenting with various trading strategies. When this happens, few of them remember to concentrate on money management strategies, yet they are just as important as well. Only when you have a sound and balanced system of managing your money will the risks of the positions you want to open and be reduced. Track each cent you invest in the trade and keep your books to know when a business works for you and not for proper decision-making.

Simultaneously executing too many trades

Many traders make the error of believing that more transactions result in more earnings. But when you run too many trades at the same time, what happens is that you're going to end up hurting your investment strategy, and it could all become so confusing. Just because you have managed to beat the market a few times, don't be overconfident. You also want to stay focused even if you fail in a position you have opened up expectantly.

Operating on too small an investment

Binary options brokers usually impose the minimum investment amount, but this is not the limit set; you can invest as much as you want in binary options. You limit the chances of making a profit from your efforts when you end up underfunding the account. It is better to fund the account reasonably for a better and balanced money management strategy, not just the minimum deposit required by your broker.

Having impractical expectations

The returns you receive from your binary options investment may not always be as good as you expect them to be, and you need to be ready for bad days. This trading platform offers excellent returns, but you should define your trading goals and then work patiently to achieve them. Never expect too much because you are likely to make undirected investments then.

How Options Prices are Determined

There are many distinct expiration months and strike prices available when looking at an option chain. So how does the price of each option contract determine it?

Quite merely, choices are priced on odds. These probabilities are calculated, the Black Scholes Pricing Model being the most well-known, using various pricing methods.

What makes up the price, then? Several factors affect an option's price.

Those factors are:

- The underlying security price
- The strike price
- Time until expiration
- The volatility of the underlying protection
- Any outstanding dividends
- The current risk-free interest rate.

Let's look at the first variable more closely: the price of the underlying security.

This parameter is the simplest variable to understand, as most investors can easily visualize the relationship. The option price will change correspondingly as the value of the stock increases or decreases.

The option strike price is the second variable to consider. This parameter represents the price at which the choice can be exercised. The closer the stock price is to the strike price, the more costly the alternative is. When the stock and strike price are equal, the option's time value component is the greatest.

The amount of time until expiration is the third variable. This variable is simple to understand, the more time an option has, the greater the option's price. The closer an option gets to the expiry date, the faster it decreases the time value. On expiration, the time value component of the option premium will be worth 0.

Only the time value component of an option decays, to emphasize, and any intrinsic value remains intact, only affected by a move in the underlying security.

The fourth variable, the volatility of the underlying security, is implied. This parameter is a crucial component of the option's price because it adjusts over the life of the option for the anticipated price movement. Stock options that are more likely to make a big move are more expensive than options for slower-moving, less volatile stocks.

The fifth variable in pricing is dividends. All known dividends are priced into the option's value To ensure precise pricing. This parameter equalizes the advantages of being long on the base vs. creating long synthetic positions using options alone.

Interest rates are the final variable in option pricing. The interest rate free of risk is priced into the option. This parameter is also priced into the option to equalize the advantage of long on the underlying versus using options only to create synthetic long positions.

Specific names based on the Greek alphabet have been given to all these variables and are collectively known as the 'Greeks' options. These Greeks measure the option price's sensitivity to a change in one of these variables. In our next section, we'll cover the Greeks.

Although several variables influence an option's price, a few basic principles need to be understood by the starting trader or investor.

First, let us examine the critical correlations between call options and the price of the underlying security.

Again this is the simplest variable to understand, as the call option's price will increase as the stock price increases.

Under the same principles, the call option's price will also decrease in price if the stock was to fall in value.

The impact of time decay on the price of the call option is simple. The time value component of the option value decays as more time passes.

The effect of implied volatility on the call option's price is also simple. The implied volatility increases, the cost of the call option also increases, and the call option price also decreases as the implied volatility decreases.

Let's look at the Put Options now.

Again, let's first examine the critical correlations between put options and the underlying safety price.

The price of the underlying option to the put option has an inverse connection. When a stock price rises, then the cost of the put option will decrease. Under the same principles, if the stock price's value were to fall, the price of the put option would rise in price.

Next, the relationship is identical to the call option when reviewing the effects of time decay on the put option price. The time value component of the option price decays as more time passes.

Similarly, the same simple relationship becomes evident when we look at the effects of implied volatility on the put option price. As the implied volatility increases, the cost of the put option increases as well. And as the volatility meant decreases, then the price of the put option also decreases.

Why Financial Leverage

You can use the lever as an easy mechanical tool to transmit the necessary force to accomplish a given task by using physics laws. The benefit of using a lever is that the energy force's efficiency being delivered to a particular job can be significantly increased. A teeter-totter found in a playground for children is a prime example. We have a lever here that's braced across a fulcrum. That lever was set up by two people, one at each end. Nothing happens if they are of equal weight and at an equal distance from the fulcrum. As they maintain a state of equilibrium, they cancel each other out. If one individual outweighs the other or if one individual is further from the center than the other individual, then he/she has a mechanical advantage. With the force of gravity dragging him/her, as the lighter person or person nearer to the fulcrum is raised, he/she will fall to the ground. A thirty-pound child can easily send a football player skyward by taking apparent advantage of this toy. The infant has multiplied its strength many times over.

Financial leverage is based on the same theory and provides the same benefit. Let's assume we have a certain level of company activity that we want to achieve. That level is resting low on the lever right now. Our financial net worth, exerting an absolute pressure as it seeks to send business activity up, is at the opposite end. But the energy needed to lift the business activity is more significant than that exerted on the opposite end by pushing the net worth. This scenario could be related to someone whose net worth is not good enough to get a new company off the ground. He or she needs more money, or more leverage needs to be applied.

In the application of leverage, there are basically two variables that could add weight to net worth, providing sufficient strength to accomplish the task. First, until it outweighs the company's resting strength, the size of the new value itself can be increased. The second is the role of the focal point concerning net worth and business activity. If the center of gravity is moved towards the business activity, then the net worth will increase its effective power. Or if the distance between the center of gravity and the net value pressure point is increased - by extending the length of that portion of the lever - the effective net worth force will also rise over the business activity.

The investor who wants to purchase an apartment building for one hundred thousand dollars, but only has ten thousand dollars of their funds available for the investment, is another excellent example of the application of leverage. If they are getting the building, the weight of that ten thousand must be multiplied. His/her response is to approach different lending institutions and organize the venture's execution using OPM (other people's money). Their net worth and credit rating can be used effectively to gain the necessary balance. In effect, they used the leverage of their ten thousand dollars and credit standing to multiply the initial force of investment reserve by ten, giving them the total amount necessary for the purchase when they have succeeded in obtaining these funds. Again we can see the use of financial leverage in practical terms.

What if you don't want to borrow money, or if you can't borrow money? There are types of leverage that are just as efficient in today's economy. With the idea of taking over an existing loan and paying monthly payments back to the seller on their equity, you could approach the seller. As leverage to acquire the property, you are using your ability to maintain the existing loan, which helps the seller maintain good credit. To apply pressure or influence under existing conditions, use your clout.

CHAPTER FOUR

UNDERSTANDING PASSIVE INCOME

Hundreds of thousands of internet marketers are entirely focused on passive revenue. It is the most tempting form of income by far, as it allows you to earn cash regularly, even if you are not active at work. Because of the hype generated by this notion, many individuals come up with their dream interpretations of it, and some are unfortunately missing the mark. If you decide to pursue that objective, it is better to take a closer look at it and the things you should expect.

It takes time and effort to develop Passive Income.

This passive income status overnight is doubtful to be achieved. Think of it as a missile where you need to build a lot of energy to launch it. But once it's in the air, all you need to do is make a fraction of the effort to keep things going.

The time-consuming bit is creating an actual pathway. If it were a simple thing to do instead of sticking to tedious ways of earning money, everyone would be involved. Sadly, it's not that straightforward, and you can't just create wealth from thin air. Buying a possible passive income channel is your only other alternative.

Available Passive Income Channels

Few channels are worth exploring, although it sounds a bit restrictive. Through the use of Google AdSense, the most common is. This manner is a technique that you can try free of charge, but you need to develop an excellent website designed for a specific niche. That website must have AdSense ads and must have steady traffic to ensure that the advertisements generate regular passive revenue. As long as you keep a keen eye on your progress, AdSense should keep working throughout the months.

Traffic construction can fuel other passive revenue channels, such as info products so that you can use a sales funnel set up to convert leads to sales effectively. As long as traffic continues to pour in, the revenue will not stop. Affiliate marketing also counts as a passive revenue channel as another business will manage the traffic so that once you start making sales, all you get are commissions. Even if commissions are simply a fraction of the items sold, these numbers can add up as long as your traffic is consistent.

You can conclude that there is not such a thing as 100 percent passive income because you still have to do your part. Never think of it as something that you can just turn on and wait for the cash on your payment processor to pile up. If you do not have a passion for maintaining it, even famous online entrepreneurs like Robert Kiyosaki do not recommend the whole passive income concept. Before settling down on a specific channel, plan, and make sure you gradually lay out the groundwork to create or buy your way to success.

Stock Selection

Investors should aim to capture the most value by buying stocks where future earnings growth is visible and where this growth can be purchased at a reasonable price.

A disciplined stock-picking approach

Stocks for growth

Investors should essentially seek to identify shares that are ready for a change in status, i.e., claims that are likely to be re-rated shortly. Initially, this is best done by employing stock-screening filters without industry-specific knowledge.

The Price Earnings Growth Ratio, or PEG, used to avoid overpaying for future earnings growth, is one of the most useful search criteria for identifying growth stocks.

An attractive PEG of 0.5 would, for example, be calculated by dividing the price-earnings ratio (PER) of a company or multiple earnings, say 10, by its forecast growth rate in earnings per share (EPS), say 20. In other words, the growth in earnings per share forecast by the company is twice that of the multiple payments awarded by the market to it. The larger the number of profits, the higher the expectations of the market are for growth.

One useful approach to use when searching for development shares is to combine multiple criteria. For instance, about their growth rates, you could search for stocks with a low PER, above-average EPS growth (say over 20 percent), and strong cash flow per share concerning EPS, which helps eliminate creative accounting.

Assuming that one's analysis is correct and steadily increasing its earnings to, say, 20 percent per annum, all other things being equal, the stock should maintain its rating. Its share price should rise by an appropriate 20 percent.

However, investors' expectations of growth prospects for a consistent growth-share often increase over time, and the market is likely to award a higher multiple. For example, a re-rating from eight times earnings to 12 times would have a more dramatic effect and increase the share price by 50 percent.

It is essential to note that the shift in investors' perception of a business often leads to more significant wealth creation than the actual financial results themselves.

As a result of something new,' positive earnings surprises are usually triggered, such as earnings enhancing acquisitions, positive structural, demographic or legislative change, discoveries, the introduction of disruptive technology, new product cycles, etc.

Deep Value

During an economic downturn or recession, another example of where a lot of value can be created occurs. The indiscriminate mark-down of stocks, both good and bad, usually makes this as over-leveraged investors and funds are compelled to sell their holdings.

Those inventories that are marked down in price but defy the downturn and continue to boost their earnings can become seriously undervalued. If a company's shares are indiscriminately marked down in this manner,' deep value' is likely to emerge.

CHAPTER FIVE

THE BEST STRATEGIES TO MAKE MONEY IN OPTIONS TRADING

There are good reasons to believe that trading in options is a great chance to earn money. How to make cash with options trading, on the other hand, is a different field. It can be said that options trading is not as risky when you are about to compare trading options with other stocks or securities. Some market experts even believe that not only trends or strategies but luck also lies in success or failure in options trading.

True enough, it has become highly interesting for rookie traders how to make money with options trading. They are not only interested in learning the ins and outs of the world of the market; they are also eager to earn vast amounts of profit. However, as one needs preparation and the right amount of comparative research, this feat is no easy undertaking.

Determining whether to buy a call or place an option spells initial success. Deciding on these terms will also provide you with ideas on how to make money from trading options. You have to understand which one suits your preferences and methods of trading. It helps to study the market as well.

You may decide to opt for OTM or ITM alternatives. Without necessarily depending on stock movements and underlying asset prices, OTM or out-of-the-money options generate income. You are just essentially waiting for the contract to expire and collect cash as earnings with this.

Go for long-term bonds. This parameter may lead to higher premiums being paid, but it ultimately pays well. Unlike short-term stock options, you are assured that you are not just waiting for worthless contracts to expire. Finally, you are reducing your chances of losses, as much as you are expanding the network for potential gain.

How to make money from trading options does not start and end with trading options/stocks. You could try being a writer or a bookie as well. You can also choose to earn direct cash by selling your options on the market at their current price.

It is also essential to be mindful of terms, contracts, and expiration dates in options trading. Knowing a future option agreement can, if properly understood, spell cash. Before its expiry date, you may decide to sell the option. Or you can choose to close your stocks ahead of time and immediately earn some money.

It is best to know the field you are entering and decide what is best, whether you plan to become a professional trader or want to be a normal risk-taker. By doing this as a part-time job or merely engaging in options trading as a way to increase wealth, you may be able to earn a profit. Regardless of your motives, learning is the only thing that you have to keep in mind. In other words, you have to understand the essential details and work your way through them.

Options in Index Funds

Managed funds offer higher diversification than can be achieved by direct share investing by most individuals. While there are many thousands of managed funds, "active and passive" can nearly be broken down into two groups.

By wise stock selection, actively managed funds try to outperform the benchmark index, while 'passive' managed funds try to match the benchmark index. Passive funds are known as index funds for this reason. Index funds will hold all the securities in any given index simultaneously as the index shares. For instance, if share Y represents 3% of an index, then 3% of their funds will be invested in share Y by an index fund.

Some investors run away from index funds because they are not happy with the 'average' as a return. Still, when they are made aware of index funds' advantages, they generally change their opinion.

1. Lower costs – are research costs or the high salaries and bonuses paid to some active fund managers are not incurred by an index fund. This fact means that most index funds are approximately 0.50 percent cheaper than managed funds that are active.

2. Tax Efficiencies - Stocks tend to remain in the index for a very long time, which means that index funds also hold stocks for a very long time. You never get a capital gains tax liability if you buy a stock but do not sell it. To attract new funds, compare this with an active fund manager whose main objective is to have as high a headline rate possible. There is little concern about the investor's tax situation, and it is not uncommon to see active funds sell 100% of their portfolio annually. This fact can sometimes lead to a farcical situation in which the investor has a negative return on its investment but still receives a tax bill.

3. Diversification - As the index funds invest in all of the shares in the index, the level of diversification is greater than that of active fund managers. This enhanced diversification makes it possible for an investor to limit risk, specifically unsystematic risk. This way is one of the times where, without sacrificing the return, you can reduce risk.

Irrespective of investment styles, there is always an average return on the share market. Those who outperform the average return have done so at the expense of those who have underperformed the average return. Therefore, we know that the return of the average actively managed fund will generally be equal to the return of the stock market as a whole and hence of the average index fund, before costs. Since index funds have lower fees, the assurance must be that the average index fund will always outperform the average active fund after fees.

That's why an index fund investor can be pretty sure that the average active fund manager will outperform the middle active fund manager after expenses and never underperform the active fund manager. And this happens before tax is taken into account.

Share markets move in cycles, and managed funds with a growth slant do better in bull markets, but value funds typically outperform in bear markets. While some active fund managers will beat index funds in any given year, it is scarce in subsequent years for this performance to continue. In fact, in the second year, only about 14% of the top 100 active fund managers repeated their performance in any single year between 1996 and 2006. While every fund manager thinks they can beat the index, the fact is that about 50 percent of them don't do it every year.

Candlesticks

One of the most reliable indicators that both traders and investors always use when they want to enter the decision-making position is Candlestick. This position is because the candlestick is the only indicator that follows a specific stock's movement when the market opens. When the price is closed for a certain period, it will generate one candle. Other metrics are just waiting until the candle is developed to be one, and then they follow the pattern. Here are some of the terminologies that we usually see in the graph of Candlestick Candles.

Bullish engulfing: a bullish (white) candle covers the bearish (red) candle. This parameter is what happens when the market opens; the candle opens the same or lower than the previous closing candle, and the candle closes higher than the last candle closing when the market is closed. On the uptrend, every time we see this pattern, it is confirmation for entry.

The inverse of the Bullish Engulfing pattern is Bearish Engulfing.

Doji is Indecisive, meaning at the same position, the candle is opened and closed. We need to wait each time we see this type of pattern because there is no confirmation.

The bullish Harami is shorter than the bearish (Red) candle than the bullish (White) candle. If the next candle shows gaping up on the opening candle and closing is higher than the previous closing candle on the upward trend, all you need to do is wait for the next candle. For the uptrend position, it is confirmation for entry.

The Bearish Harami is the reverse of the Bullish Harami pattern.

Time-based charts (Candlesticks, OHLC Bars and Heikin-Ashi, in particular) do not represent the price. This section will help you realize that recognizing time-based patterns is an unreliable technique for trading stock options.

Some retail training companies like to popularize the myth that Everyone looks at these patterns in the charts" They're partly correct. However, their use of the term "Everyone" refers to off-the-floor retail traders who collectively only make up a maximum of ~ 15%, in some cases even less of the total volume traded on exchanges, depending on which exchange it is.

Which brings the question: What are the eyes of those on the floor looking at moving 80+ percent of the volume traded? Some of you have visited the exchanges organized through your broker. All you'll find is rapid math notation if you've picked up the paper scattered on the floor: addition, subtraction, division, and multiplication. Nothing else anymore. No Tri-Star Doji drawings, Dumpling Tops, or Frypan Bottoms drawings. It makes sense because screens with price data and price alone are all that is in front of floor traders. Floor traders could care less about how many times during the day, with truckloads of calls and hedges, the price touched the tail of a Dragonfly Doji. They've already planned to get more of it or unload their inventory of calls/puts at a specific strike for a given price.

As a trader of retail options, you are not exempt from tuning your eyes to focus only on price, trading less than ten contracts per trade. If you delete the use of Candlesticks, OHLC Bars, and Heikin-Ashi charts, how do you simulate price observation alone from off-the-floor? Instead, use Point & Figure charts.

Why is it valid for trading options to use only Point & Figure charts? The only technique that plots only one type of data - price without time alone - price is the only element of data required on a distribution curve. This technique is the same distribution curve used by your options trading platform in the Bjerksund-Stensland, Black-Scholes, or Binomial pricing models.

What about other techniques for charting, such as Candlesticks and OHLC Bars? Let us take, as an example, the Doji, a well-known candlestick. The Doji is characterized at the same price by the Open and Close, and the High is a different price from the Low. Remember, it records the horizontal axis price with a distribution curve and the frequency on the vertical axis. It has to be flipped on to its side to map the Doji on the relevant axis of the distribution curve for the price points of the Doji to line up against the vertical axis.

Thus, a price that closes at the same price opened is recorded as two price points with the high and low frequency twice. You can not leave the lines joining the dots of the Doji on the chart with a distribution curve. All that is mapped are four dots that represent the price points of the Doji. Take the lines joining the dots away. Question: The Doji, where is it? No longer relevant. To any candlestick, the same logic applies (spinning top, hammer, etc.). Once they are mapped on to a distribution curve, candlesticks lose their features. For the OHLC method used to check fractals in Elliot

Waves and wave counts, the waves lose their characteristics once the price is mapped in its dispersion mode. The implication is the same.

Follow the link at the end of this section, entitled Candlesticks/OHLC Charts Lose their Patterns on a Distribution Curve, to visualize this problem with time-based charts.

Does a charting method need to be reconciled with the distribution curve? Yes, one Standard Deviation (σ) equals 68 percent. -/+1σ sets the probability parameters that you build an option spread around to test whether or not the strikes will be touched, from the date a spread is filled to its expiry date.

Bear in mind, transforming the time frames in time-based charts from minute/hour/day/week to reconcile conflicting patterns in one-time structure with another. Whether it be Candlesticks, Heikin-Ashi, OHLC, it does nothing to help you work out the Theta as a decline in a debit spread; or the positive Theta as a premium sold in a credit spread. The expiration date is the only unit of time needed to feed into a Theoretical Pricing Model, which in turn affects the probabilities per day for the number of days that pass. It makes no sense to use them because the units of time in time-based charts have no value in theoretically pricing an option.

So what are time-based charts (Candlesticks, Heikin-Ashi, and OHLC Bars) useful for? They help trade the underlying thing itself. In addition to dealing with +/- Delta (directional risk), all the other

Greeks (Gamma, Theta and Vega) are equal to zero when you trade the underlying itself. Time-based charts are relevant as a surrogate to the product for purely directional trading of the underlying itself for trading deep ITM options.

The deeper the ITM you reach, the wider the Bid-Ask spread is compared to the narrower differences in the Bid-Ask Spread's ATM or OTM strikes. Do you have enough capital in the account to keep trading only on ITM strikes? This is why many retail traders with account sizes under USD $25K are looking for lower-priced products to increase, for example, $20 and below, as they are looking for ITM strikes that are affordable for them trade using Candlestick/OHLC/Heikin-Ashi charts.

These products often suffer illiquid open interest in their strikes because of their lower prices, making you chase price for an uncompetitive filling, only to result in poor price-profit performance. The other extreme is to over-spend on ITM strikes of a higher-priced product, such as $100 and above, as you found a business candidate using some "special" pattern scanning software, only to fill the order in violation of the money management rule of 2%-5% per trade.

CHAPTER SIX

POSITION ANALYSIS

Recently, without any mention or introduction to technical analysis, almost no trading seminar options are available. Nearly all of the blog trading options on the Internet use technical analysis as their primary decision-making basis. Why is it so? Why is the trading of options now so closely related to technical analysis?

We need first to know what technical analysis does in the first place to understand the critical relationship between technical analysis and options trading.

Two main analysis methods are available: Fundamental Analysis and Technical Analysis.

Fundamental analysis is reading a business or economy's essential data to predict and invest in the business or market's future performance. Profit and loss statement invoice, earnings growth, and earnings guidance are such fundamental information. The issue with basic analysis is that big business do not always make great stocks. Stocks of large businesses, often for extended periods, also experience periods of downturn. As such a fundamental analysis, if nothing unpredictable happens to the company in the years down the road, it mostly helps an investor to decide what stocks to buy for the long term (5 to 10 years out). The simple analysis is a useful tool for investors buying stocks for their dividends and dividend growth.

Technical analysis (TA) is the analysis of stock market data. Yes, while Fundamental Analysis is a company's research, TA exclusively studies its stock. Such market data includes the price and volume transacted over different periods. Options traders see from price and volume how a stock's price is doing regardless of what the company data is doing. This fact helps speculators and investors avoid those extended downturn periods even though their necessary information looks great. Indeed, while the fundamental analysis tells an investor which business is doing well when it is time to buy or sell its stocks, TA tells an investor. The technical analysis's strength is to guide investors' buying and sell decisions through price patterns and price trends over short periods.

So why in options trading, is technical analysis such a favorite?

It should be recalled that fundamental analysis is favorable for long-term investment and that technical analysis is advantageous even for short periods. Stock traders may hold stocks forever, but after a fixed time, options expire! Yes, options last no more than a year, and options traders regularly use options trading strategies in months or weeks requiring extremely short outlooks. This way is precisely why technical analysis is associated so closely with the trading of options. Traders of options do not have the luxury of maintaining a position for years as stock traders do.

On top of that, traders of options do not get dividends as stock investors do. In options trading, the only way to make money is for the expected outlook to play out within the options' expiration period. This fact makes the necessary strength of the business on which it is based relatively unimportant. On top of that, when stocks also fall, options traders can profit. This fact also makes it relatively unimportant to identify good firms through fundamental analysis.

Indeed, reading price trends and price trends that could show the direction a stock is moving the next week or month has more value to trading options than reading a profit and loss statement from a company that doesn't tell you where its stock may go at all for the short term.

Before Entering an Exchange

1-Is this a set-up of high quality; does it fit the trade criteria I want?

Over-trading is a simple trap to fall into, but you can potentially avoid unnecessary losses by checking out the right boxes as to what qualifies as a fair trade set-up each time before you enter the market. It is considered a win to avoid a bad loss; you have to return one less loss.

Whether it's physical, digital, or mental, using a checklist can be an excellent way to keep you on the right track. It helps you ensure that you only take those set-ups that meet your game plan's criteria.

2. Where can I enter?

That question is connected with question #1, but with a twist. Your set-ups are potential opportunities, but there are various ways to take advantage of those possibilities. For example, if you are trading price levels, will you enter right at a price or wait for a reaction and use, say, before entering, a candlestick formation?

Another illustration. Perhaps you prefer breakouts or pullbacks to trade. An extensive trading range could form, then sudden breakout-some traders will buy the breakout, others will wait for a retreat or a combination of the two following the breakout. To personal preference, this comes down.

Are you going to scale in at various points as the market moves in a specific way? A common way to enter and exit is via multiple entries. Know exactly how you want to join in any event.

3-Where do I exit?

If the trade goes for and against you, you must know where you will exit; profit targets and stop-losses. Before you enter the business, this needs to be determined, not after. Stop-losses should be from the point where it is most likely that you are proven wrong. Based on past price action, support and resistance levels provide potential entry and exit levels for traders. These are levels that have been respected and need to be recognized in any trading strategy. For instance, placing a stop on a long-trade sufficiently below support is logical.

If the trade is profitable, where are you going to leave? What is your goal? This fact should be based, for technical traders, on sound analysis. If you are long, for instance, where are the next levels of resistance? Where are the following classes of support if it's short?

In either case, assigning fixed values is not prudent (i.e., I will risk 'x number of pips to make 'x' number) for stop-loss and profit goals. You are imposing your right on the market in this situation and not using logical levels based on the analysis.

4-Based on questions 2 and 3, what is my risk/reward?

The distance based on entry to stop-loss and range based on access to target determines your risk/reward ratio. This manner should once again be based on logical analysis. You want to look for asymmetrical possibilities where your reward outweighs your risk significantly.

A great rule of thumb is a 1:2 risk/reward ratio, but it depends on your trading strategy. For example, the win/loss percentage will be lower for traders who employ breakout or momentum strategies, but the risk/reward profile will be more significant. On the other hand, a much higher win/loss percentage, but with lower risk/reward ratios, will have range-trading or mean-reversion strategies. You want to have a positive skew between the amount risked and the possible profit in either case.

5-How much capital am I prepared to risk?

Understand your risk tolerance and trade accordingly with position-sizing. This fact varies from one trader to the next. It is best to think about how much you will risk rather than straight leverage in terms of percentage of risk capital per trade, i.e., 0.25 percent, 0.5 percent, 1 percent, 2 percent, etc.). Your position-size and leverage factor will be dynamic Meaning, depending on the distance from entry to stop-loss.

The position-size also depends on the time frame and frequency you are operating in. For example, given the low frequency of trades, a swing-trader holding days to weeks may risk larger amounts than, say, a day-trader, who can make numerous trades in a single session. In the latter case, it is prudent to attempt a far smaller amount, as losses can add up very quickly.

6-I have a high conviction level; can I accept a loss?

This fact is the final question without hesitation that needs to be answered. You are attempting to align the objective with the subjective here. You should feel good and be confident about the trade you are about to enter, giving you the best opportunity to properly manage the business once the P&L begins to move around.

Due to a high level of uncertainty, it will be easy to fall prey to careless errors if you do not have a proper conviction level. Such careless mistakes will lead to frustration, and more frustration can be caused by frustration. A vicious cycle which you would like to avoid.

CHAPTER SEVEN

TRADING IN OPTIONS AND OTHER FINANCIAL INSTRUMENTS

Financial instruments are described as assets that can be traded or viewed as capital packages that can be traded. Most types of financial instruments ensure the efficient flow and transfer of capital to investors worldwide. Such assets may be cash, the contractual right to deliver or receive some money, another type of financial instrument, or proof of the entity's ownership.

- A financial instrument is a virtual document containing any kind of monetary value representing a legal agreement.

- It is possible to split financial instruments into two types: cash instruments and derivative instruments.

- Financial instruments may also be split by an asset class, depending on whether they are debt-based or equity-based.

- A third unique type of financial instrument is comprised of foreign exchange instruments.

Understanding Financial Instruments

Virtual documents that represent a legal agreement involving any sort of monetary value can be financial instruments. Financial instruments based on equity represent the ownership of an asset. Debt-based financial instruments represent a loan to the owner of the investment made by an investor.

A third unique type of financial instrument is comprised of foreign exchange instruments. There are various subcategories of every device, such as preferred share equity and common share equity.

Financial instruments are defined by International Accounting Standards (IAS) as any contract that gives rise to a financial asset of one entity and a financial liability or equity instrument of another entity."

Financial Instruments Types

It is possible to split financial instruments into two types: cash instruments and derivative instruments.

Cash Instruments

- Cash instruments' values are directly influenced and determined by the markets. These may be readily transferable securities.
- Deposits and loans agreed by borrowers and lenders may also be cash instruments.

Instruments for Derivatives

- The value and features of derivative instruments are based on the vehicle's underlying components, such as assets, interest rates, or indices.

For example, an equity options contract is a derivative because it derives its value from its underlying stock. The option gives the right to buy or sell the stock at a specified price and a specific date, but not the obligation. As the stock price increases and decreases, so do the option's value, although not necessarily by the same percentage.

Derivatives or exchange-traded derivatives may be over-the-counter (OTC). OTC is a market or method in which securities are priced and traded and not listed on formal exchanges.

Types of Financial Instruments Asset Classes

It is also possible to divide financial instruments according to an asset class, which depends on whether they are debt-based or equity-based.

Financial Instruments Based on Debt

These instruments are short-term financial instruments based on debt last for one year or less. So securities of this sort come in the form of commercial paper and T-bills. Cash of this kind may be deposits and deposit certificates (CDs).

Exchange-traded derivatives can be short-term interest rate futures under short-term, debt-based financial instruments. Forward rate agreements are OTC derivatives.

Long-term financial instruments are based on debt last for more than a year. These are bonds with securities. Loans are cash equivalents. Bond futures and options on bond futures are exchange-traded derivatives. Interest rate swaps, interest rate caps, interest rate options, interest rate floors, and exotic products are OTC derivatives.

Equity-based financial tools

Equity-based financial instrument securities are stocks. Then exchange-traded derivatives include stock options and equity futures in this category. Stock options and exotic products are OTC derivatives.

Securities on foreign exchange are not available. In spot foreign exchange, which is the new prevailing rate, cash equivalents occur. Currency futures are exchange-traded derivatives under foreign exchange. In foreign exchange options, outright forward and foreign exchange swaps, OTC derivatives occur.

Although it can be very profitable for trading derivatives such as options and futures, it may not be for those unable to deal with risks. These are regarded as advanced investment types, so it must be severe for those who would like to trade using these tools. Trading options or trading futures may not be found for those who are used to less risky investments such as bonds or stocks. They must take higher levels of risks involved and deal with the losses they may face.

However, traders who dare to take more risks may indeed be protecting their long-term investments. For example, options may be a form of hedging that helps them in a dip in the stocks or indexes they have invested. On the other hand, firms may be useful for those who would like to diversify their trading portfolios as an alternative investment. However, traders must understand that they cannot afford to sit around and wait for a long time, unlike long-term investments. As the assets being traded are time-bound, they have to deal with deadlines.

Derivatives may not indicate ownership of the underlying assets, but as with call options on stocks or indexes, financial instruments serve as a promise for traders to convey license. On the other hand, future contracts are agreements between traders based on a fixed price and on a specific date to buy or sell a certain quantity and quality of a commodity. Traders do not have to invest large amounts of money, but they can earn a profit because of price movements in the market. They don't have to buy the commodities or assets per se, but they can trade at a fraction of a price that represents a specified volume.

One of the benefits of options is that traders can opt for strategies that are conservative or speculative. Based on their trading situations, they can get into a position. Traders can use derivatives to protect their investments from market price fluctuations while increasing their profit from their current stock holdings. Options also give them the chance to earn from price increases without necessarily buying enormous stock or commodity volumes. Options and futures may also be a way for traders to profit from whatever direction market prices will take.

Significant Differences Between Futures and Options Trading

Options and futures trading are contracts between two traders. Some people consider these investment options quite risky, but it is possible to make a profit with proper understanding and planning. Investors need to understand all the risks involved in these investment decisions at the same time. A financial instrument's future price, such as a bond, stock, or commodity, is fixed in options trading. One trader agrees to sell while another trader agrees to purchase the specific item on the predetermined date at the fixed price.

If the share is trading at a higher price on the options contract's predetermined date, then the investor purchases the share at the agreed price and makes a profit. However, if the share is sold on a predetermined date at a lower price, the investor can decide not to buy it. The investor has to pay an option price in both cases. There are two forms of contracts for options - calls and puts. The first is generally purchased in the hope that the price will increase. If the investor expects the price to decrease in the future, the put options are usually bought.

Trading in futures is considered somewhat riskier than trading in options. The buying trader is obliged to purchase the contract in the futures trade. Generally, the terms are standard and fixed. The buying trader can decide to take physical delivery of the assets in this type of trading, go for the monetary settlement, or choose the agreement's opposite.

One party faces higher risk in futures trading because both the buyer and the seller have an obligation on the settlement date to sell or buy the assets at a fixed price. Unlike trading options, where a premium has to be paid, futures trading does not require any advance expenditure from the buyer. The asset size in it is generally quite enormous. This trading type is considered to be more volatile. Still, many investors prefer to deal in it because both parties will know the assets that would be sold and purchased in the future. It typically involves a cash settlement and not the actual exchange of goods in the case of a commodity. There are some essential considerations concerning both investment options, and it is necessary to know about them.

After understanding the trends, it is better to trade. Only if there is a chance of making a profit should the investment be made? According to the trading plan, one must prevent any emotional attachment and work. As well as exit and entry points, such a program should have reasonable goals. Compared to the other investment options available in the financial market, this type of investment is a riskier proposition. This manner makes only the spare money necessary to be used, losing which will not cause any financial problem. It is essential to evaluate all the reward and risk options properly. There are some powerful instruments and techniques that can be used To avoid losses. Investors are advised not to over-trade when it comes to options and futures trading.

Trading futures and options can be a risky business and should only be undertaken with risk capital that will not alter your lifestyle if you lose your investment. The profit potential is almost unlimited, while the loss potential is almost equally unlimited. This fact means that if you are on the losing end of a naked futures trade, you can stand to lose more cash than you have in the margin and you are responsible for the entire contract amount because of the highly leveraged nature of the investment. There are many ways to limit your risk, and one of these is to use options as a hedge away from your position, whether on the long side or the short side, against an adverse price movement. Let's take a look at few distinctions between trading futures and options.

While I said that there is almost unlimited downside potential, if you sell that choice without holding an opposite position, this is only true for an option. So if you were to sell a gold option placed in June 900 and the market went to 800, you are responsible for the 100 points against your position that the gold contract has gone against. The difference would be your loss minus the premium you collected for selling the gold. You should figure out how much you are willing to risk on any one trade and then open an opposite position to minimize your downside risk due to the volatile nature of the markets. This can be done with both trading futures and options.

Differences Between Trading Futures and Options

1. Premium versus margin

Options: You are not required to put up any margin when you purchase an option because you are buying the option at a fixed price, also known as the premium. If the underlying commodity price moves against your position or remains flat, this premium can decline over the option's life. You may lose the premium you paid for if the option is not exercised before expiration, and the seller of the option will profit from the amount of the compensation paid.

Futures: While the premium for a future option will waste time, futures contracts will not. The margin on a futures contract can be thought of as earnest cash that will make you responsible for the futures contract's full amount. This way is very risky if there is no opening of an offsetting position to protect you from an adverse price move.

2. Risk

Options: As a buyer of options, you are limited only to the amount of the premium you paid for the option, so your risk is considered limited.

Futures: You are responsible for more than just the original margin you were required to set up to make the trade, regardless of whether you buy a futures contract or sell a futures contract. This way makes this type of risk unlimited for business.

3. Dates of Expiration

The expiration date of each specific contract is one last notable difference between futures and options trading. You should know that this must be delivered about one month before the underlying futures are set to be provided if you were to exercise an option to control the underlying futures contract. This way is for the physical delivery of the commodity. It does not apply to indices that are not physical commodities and enables expiration dates to be the same as delivery dates.

As you can see concerning each contract's technical aspects, there are several fundamental differences between futures and trading options. In terms of trading platforms and specialized risk management techniques, these instruments' trading is quite another matter. For further studies on futures trading, use this section as a basic primer and see if futures and options trading is right for you.

Why Trade Future and Options?

Futures and options are categorized under the financial instruments category of derivatives. In the recent past, derivatives have been in operation since time immemorial and have become more popular. This way, even though they have been faced with a lot of criticism, they make the markets prone to instability due to a lack of transparency.

The benefit of futures and options trading is that risk management is improved, and liquidity levels are raised simultaneously. The value of futures and options is based on another asset, known as the underlying asset. It can be a stock or an index of the market.

A derivative that gives one the right to purchase or sell the underlying asset is an option. No obligation exists. There are two types of options: the option to call and the option to place. The variance between the two options is that while the put option is vested with the right to sell the underlying asset, the call option gives the investor the right to buy the asset.

A mutual agreement is known as an option contract that provides the price for the underlying asset to be purchased and sold. The option agreement also gives the expiry date when the deal will no longer be valid. In American and European styles, options can be exercised. The option can be exercised before the expiry of the contract in the American manner, while the options can be exercised during the expiry date in the European style.

Futures refer to a standardized and tradable contract, which requires settlement at specified prices and dates. Futures are riskier than options because they have a purchasing obligation. Commodities such as gold and crude oil may also be used to settle the transaction.

In several ways, trading in futures can be done. These include squaring off, which implies taking the agreement's reverse option— delivery option, where the asset is delivered physically. For example, if the sale of a specific amount of gold was involved in your future guide, then at the agreed time, you give the real gold to the buyer. Cash settlement has to do with paying the difference between the asset's future and spot price on cash terms.

A futures trading guide is essential to any person as it allows one to understand the trade rules because one can obtain a profit based on the speculation of the price movements in futures trading. For instance, when you buy futures for 3700 and sell at 4100, a gain of 400 can be achieved. The futures trading guide allows one to know that caution is needed for this trade because it involves calculated bets on the asset's movements. Studies on both the derivative and underlying assets are also vital. The changes in the underlying price impact the investment, so futures trading guides must know how to trade futures.

CHAPTER EIGHT

POINTS OF INTEREST FOR OPTIONS

TRADING

In stock option trading, there is more than just buying and selling contracts.

If you're thinking about going into trading or dabbling in it right now, here are some common issues that arise every day in trading stock options.

And these aren't merely questions of theory. At some point during your stock options trading career, each one represents a decision you will have to make. Answer wrong, and the odds are good that you will find yourself out of the money more times than you want to be.

Give a quick quiz to yourself. Do you know the best answer to the Top 12 Questions about Trading Options?

- When are you getting your premium? And does your premium receipt mean that you are in the money?"

- Should your broker charge you interest when you write Puts? If you write Puts?

- What are the Naked Puts and Covered Calls difference?

- Is there a reason why you should write Covered Calls instead of Naked Puts?

- When should you write Secured Puts for Cash? And when do you ever have to write to them?

- When selling Covered Calls, how do you factor in Time Decay?

- What's the best stock options strategy for Naked Puts hedging?

- Should you ever close the Early Naked Put?

- What's the best stock options strategy for stop-loss trading?

- Does re-investing dividends make sense?

- How does your cost basis affect reinvested dividends?

- What type of trading strategy includes the sale of Covered Puts?

All of the questions have answers that are simple but significant. And what makes the difference between an options trading expert and someone who is simply throwing money into the market and hoping for the best is knowing those answers.

Many traders like to use more sophisticated options strategies in their trading, but the fairest trade for the market situation is the simple call options trade. To increase your likelihood of profiting from call option trading, follow the steps below.

1. Determine that the price is going up for the underlying instrument. Call options trading is a directional strategy. This means that you have to choose the market direction, and the market

should move up to profit. There are many different ways in which upward market movement can be anticipated. Some individuals react to good market news, and some use basic data such as increasing earnings per share, increasing dividend yield, increasing revenue, etc. Some use chart patterns, such as the double bottom, reverse head, shoulder, ascending triangle, and upside price breakout, to indicate upward market movement. Some utilize other systems, such as Elliot waves, and systems that use price pattern combinations and other indicators.

2. Determine the price movement's target. A target price for the activity should also be indicated by the system that you use to show an upward price movement.

3. To move to your target price, anticipate the time for the underlying price. How long do you expect the cost of the underlying tools to move to the target price? To determine the expiry of the call options you wish to trade, this is essential.

4. Look at the string of options. To see the quotes and other relevant data, bring out the options chains. Nowadays, chains of real-time options are easily accessible through the internet. To get this information, you can also call your broker.

5. Narrow down to the date of exchange and expiry. If you trade online, determine the business to be submitted for your order. Based on the time you expect the price to move, choose a suitable expiration date. Usually, unless you use a trading system that trades

options near their expiry, you would like to buy call options with an expiry that is slightly longer than the expected time. This fact is to decrease the effect of time decay. This fact is very significant because time decay can lead to a loss of value for your call options.

6. For several strike rates of the same expiry, compare the Delta, Gamma, Vega, and Theta. After you have narrowed down your options chain to the specific exchange and specific expiration date, you look at the Greeks. Ideally, you would like to have high Delta, high Gamma, low Vega, and low Theta. When the underlying instrument's price moves up, High Delta and High Gamma can give you a more significant and faster profit. Low Vega is very critical when you're buying options. Low Vega implies cheaper options, and you make profits even if the underlying price does not move when Vega increases. The low volatility and quiet market are associated with Low Vega. And Low Theta means that due to time decay, the call option causes smaller losses. You can choose out-of-the-money call options if you are a longer-term trader. Such alternatives have a smaller delta but are cheaper. If you are a shorter-term trader, because they can give you faster and higher profits due to higher Delta and Gamma, you would prefer at-the-money or in-the-money call options.

7. Based on your target price, assess your risk versus rewards. You can also use a risk profile to assist you in making the assessment.

Use this formula to calculate the breakeven point: breakeven = call strike + call premium

8. Look at the interest and volume that is open. In an active market, it is better to trade so that you can easily purchase and sell. Another reason is that on the bid/ask spread, and you don't lose a lot.

9. Select the best option for the call with the highest profit probability.

10. Determine the exit point and prevent loss. Before you place in your trade, make sure you have your profit taking points and stop-loss points in place. Do this so that your emotions do not take over your decision-making after you put in your trade.

11. Place your trade-in. Call your broker online or key in your trade.

12. Watch the price movement of the underlying instrument and the price response of the option.

13. Close your stance. If you have made a profit, close your position by either selling your purchased call options or exercising the call option and selling the shares. It is usually better to sell the call options if there is some time remaining before expiry because there is still time value. If you have made a loss by selling the call options, close your position.

Credit Diffusion Strategy

If you have been trading options for a while, you may have come across a credit spread strategy for one option. Somehow, credit spread appears to be a popular strategy because it has been touted as a means for traders to consistently make money from the market by taking advantage of time decay.

At this point, I think it is crucial to align our understanding of the credit spread to avoid doubt. So what is the spread of credit? It is essentially an options strategy to be developed with the same expiration month by either using put options or call options. "This approach is part of the family of "vertical spread."

If a trader is bullish on the underlying stock or index, at a higher strike, he/she may sell a put option and buy a put option at the same time at a lower strike with the same expiration month. Conversely, if a trader is bearish on the underlying stock or index at a lower strike, he/she may sell a call option and purchase a call option at the same time at a higher strike with the same expiration month.

Based on my coaching experience, the ideas of trading credit spreads fascinated quite a number of them because they seem to believe that their brokers would pay them for initiating new credit spreads. It sounds like "risk-free trades," doesn't it? This way is partly due to the word "credit," which indicates that a trader can receive free money from his/her brokers in the above context.

Sadly, this is not the case because there is no such thing called a credit spread in the options world known by market makers. There is no free lunch, and when initiating a new options position, no traders will be paid. In reality, if I were to use "credit spread," my mentors would scold me because the correct terminology for them is "selling a put spread." Suppose we are bullish on the underlying stock or index or "selling a call spread" if we are bearish on the underlying stock or index.

What's my point here? In reality, the answer is that a credit spread is a debit spread and a credit spread is a debit spread. No brokers will pay their customers to sell a call spread or a put spread (and that means other traders and me). The truth is that if it goes dead wrong, our brokers will charge us a margin that substantially represents the maximum risk of the spread.

Did you hear about the synthetic connection in the trading of options? You should, if not. It is possible to construct all "credit" put/call synthetically spreads as "debit" call/ put spreads because of the artificial relationship. Let us use a hypothetical stock - XYZ, currently trading at $360 per share, to go through the following example.

Suppose, on XYZ, we're bullish. A 355-350 put spread (i.e., selling 1 x 355 set and buying 1 x 350 put simultaneously) can be sold at, say, $0.60. In this case, the maximum trade reward is $0.60 with a $4.40 (i.e., $5.00 - $0.60) margin. Due to the synthetic relationship, by buying a 350-355 call spread (i.e., buying 1 x 350 call and simultaneously selling 1 x 355 call) for $ 4.40, we should create the same position, which means that the maximum reward will be $ 0.60.

Exotic Options

The classes of options contracts with structures and features that differ from plain-vanilla options are exotic options (e.g., American or European options). Exotic options differ in their expiry dates, exercise prices, payoffs, and underlying assets from periodic options. Compared to the valuation of plain-vanilla options, all the features make the valuation of exotic options more sophisticated. A list of different exotic options is provided below.

The Exotic Options Explanation

The more advanced and complex features of exotic options enable substantial returns to be achieved by their holders. The various characteristics of exotic options also make them perfect for hedging and risk management.

Exotic options are financial engineering products concerned with creating new securities and the development of appropriate pricing methods. Finance experts working on the growth of new types of securities are referred to as financial engineers.

Exotic Option Types

The most popular kinds of exotic alternatives include the following:

1. Choices from Asia

One of the most commonly encountered types of exotic options is the Asian alternative. They are option contracts whose payoffs are determined over several predetermined periods by the average price of the underlying security.

2. Choices to Barrier

The exotic options barrier's main feature is that contracts are only activated if the underlying asset price reaches a predetermined level.

3. Basket Options

The options for the basket are based on several underlying assets. Essentially, the payoff of a basket option is the weighted average of all underlying assets. Note that the underlying asset weights are not always equal.

4. Options for Bermuda

These are a combination of options that are American and European. Like the European options, it is possible to exercise the Bermuda options at the date of their expiry. At the same time, these exotic options are also exercisable between purchase and expiry dates at predetermined dates.

5. Binary Choices

Digital options are also referred to as binary options. Based on the occurrence of a particular event, the options ensure the payoff. The payoff is a fixed amount or a predetermined asset if the event has occurred. Conversely, the profit is nothing if the event has not happened. In other words, only all-or-nothing gains are provided by binary options.

6. Chooser Options

Chooser's exotic choices give the holder the right to decide whether calls or puts are the options purchased. Note that it is only possible to decide on a fixed date before the expiry of the contracts.

7. Compound Choices

Compound options are essentially an option on an option (also known as split-fee options). This option's final payoff depends on the profit of another option. For this reason, there are two expiry dates and two strike prices for compound options.

8. Extendable Choices

Contracts for extendable options provide the right to postpone their expiration dates. For instance, if the options are out-of-money, the holder-extendable options allow a buyer to extend their options by a predetermined amount of time. Conversely, the writer-extendable options provide a writer (issuer) with options with similar rights.

9. Choices for Lookback

Lookback options do not initially have a specified exercise price, unlike other types of options. However, on the maturity date, the holder of the lookback options has the right to choose among the costs that have occurred during the options' lifetime, the most favorable strike price.

10. Options to Spread

The difference between the prices of the two underlying assets depends on the payoff of the spread option.

11. Options for range

Their final payoff also characterizes the options for the range. The final profit of the exotic range of options is defined as the spread over the lifetime of the options between the maximum and minimum prices of the underlying asset.

Trading in Forex options has come a long way since it began. Before, only over the counter can transactions be carried out (OTC). Today that is not the norm anymore. While OTC deals still exist, the most common way to do forex trading, including trading currency options, is to use laptops and computers and telephones/cell phones via the internet.

Trading currency options is just one of the many kinds of financial market trading done in the vast world called the Foreign Exchange market. Indeed, Forex has been the world's largest financial market and has been like that for decades. At present, every single day, billions of dollars are traded in it. Two basic types of options are traded in forex options trading, and the aliases, Vanilla options, and Exotic options are given.

Vanilla Option or just Vanilla is the informal but commonly used terminology assigned to a standard option of any financial tool, not only a currency option. If the word "vanilla" is placed before "option," then the usual type of option is that particular option, which involves only the simplest meaning of options, the strike price, and the expiry date. Vanilla options in forex are defined as either a standard call option or a typical put option being purchased and sold. The term vanilla allows the trader to immediately acknowledge that the option at hand is just the standard one since there are more complex options.

The Exotic options, on the other hand, are more complicated in structure. Commonly, this type is transacted over the counter. If the date, price, and payout structure are precise and specific in the Vanilla option, one or all of these features may vary in the exotic option. This fact is based on the fact that the broker tailors this option according to the trader's requirements.

Why Trade Exotic Options

Exotic options have unique underlying circumstances that make them a good fit for high-level active portfolio management and solutions specific to the situation. These derivatives' complex pricing may give rise to arbitrage, providing sophisticated quantitative investors with great opportunities. Arbitrage is the purchase and sale simultaneously of an asset to exploit the differences in financial instruments' price.

For a smaller premium than a comparable vanilla option, an exotic option can be purchased in many cases. The lower costs are often due to the extra features that increase the likelihood of a worthless option expiring. Nevertheless, there are exotic-style choices that are more costly than their traditional counterparts, such as chooser choices, for example, since the "choice" increases the likelihood of closing the option in-the-money. While the chooser may be more expensive than a single vanilla option, if a big move is expected, it could be cheaper than buying both a vanilla call and put, but the trader is unsure of the direction.

Exotic options may also be appropriate for companies that need to hedge an underlying asset up to or down to specific price levels. Hedging includes placing an offsetting position or investment in a security or portfolio to offset adverse price movements. For instance, because they come into existence or go out of existence at specific barrier price levels, barrier choices can be a useful hedging tool.

A Real-World Example of Exotic Option

Say, for instance, an investor owns Apple Inc. equity shares (AAPL). The investor bought the stock at $150 per claim and wants to safeguard the position if the stock falls.

With a strike price of $150, the investor buys a Bermuda-style put option that expires in three months. Since one option contract equals 100 shares, the option premium costs $2, or $200.

The option protects the stock position for the next three months from a price decline below $150. However, there is an exotic feature of this Bermuda option that allows the investor to exercise early on the first of each month until expiry.

The stock price declines to $100 in month one, and the investor exercises the put option by the first day of the option's second month. The investor is selling Apple shares at $100 per share. However, the strike price of $150 for the put option pays a $50 gain to the investor. Including the stock position and putting the $150 minus the $2 premium paid for the put, the investor has left the whole place.

If Apple's stock price increased after the option was exercised in month two, say to $200 by the expiration date of the option, by selling the position in month two, the investor would have missed out on the profits.

Although exotic options provide flexibility and customization, they do not guarantee that the investor's choices and choices whose strike price, expiry date, or whether or not to exercise early will be correct or profitable.

CHAPTER NINE

KEYS TO SUCCESS

Stock option trading gives the qualified trader more potential than almost any other online trading form in today's market to trade a fortune option. The degree of controlled risk with superior leverage allows a knowledgeable option trader the opportunity to make huge profits. Still, to have long-term success in options trading, an aspiring options trader must have a solid foundation of education about what makes up a sound options trading method. When developing a winning stock options system, there are five essential keys that any options trader must understand.

First, the degree to which time affects the premium of the option you consider trading must be understood. When factoring time into stock option trading decisions, there are two components that you must consider. The first thing you need to consider is the intrinsic time left for an option. Because options have a limited period of anywhere from 30 days to several years depending on the specific option you purchased, you need to make sure that you buy the right option with enough time on it. This way ensures that time decay does not erode your investment before your position has enough time frame to be profitable.

The second skill of profitably trading options is to factor time into your trading system to trade a specific stock option and understand the statistics of your options trading methodology or options trading setup by knowing the average trade signal holding period. If your average holding time for an options trade is seven days, you don't want to buy an option with a three-month time premium left on it because, with the purchase price of the option, you would pay more for the extra time. Nor would you purchase an option less than 30 days before expiry as time decay would erode the option value so quickly that even if the option's underlying stock movement moved favorably to you. The time decay would prevent you from realizing a gain in the option itself.

The third thing about profitable trading of options is understanding the volatility relationship between the market, the underlying stock underlying the stock option, and the effect on the value of the option itself. When the entire stock market as an index that goes through volatility periods or low trading ranges, the stocks that make up the market tend to follow the overall trend and begin to experience periods of low overall volatility that can result in cheap or low premiums derivatives as stock options. But if the market volatility increases, it is likely that individual stocks will follow the trend causing stock option premiums to increase in value as the market moves in favor of the trader. The next key to successfully trading stock options is to have a stock option trading method that considers these critical factors. Simultaneously, giving clear entry signals, clear exit signals, a defined trading management system, and a profit factor more significant than your average loss over a series of trades. If you do not have a trading methodology that guides you in every step of the trading process, knowing the ins and outs of different trade setups is useless. A robust trading method holds you by the hand and describes each step, leading you to be a consistent market winner and a profitable trader when everything is said and done.

Finally, yourself, especially your trading psychology, is the fifth and final key to successfully trading stock options. Human beings and their mental makeup are very complex, so stock options traders must have a sound trading methodology for stock options and the discipline to follow their trading methods. You can give the same winning trading scheme to two individuals, but it is widespread for them to have specific results. Invariably, the one who can stay as detached from his losing trades and his winning trades while preserving the discipline to follow the rules of the system irrespective of the trading outcome will eventually emerge as the greatest winner.

Using these five keys to develop your stock options trading methodology can help you avoid many starting option traders' errors and pitfalls. You now have a foundation to develop into a winning stock options trader by understanding time decay. Factoring an option's time into your trading method, how volatility affects a stock option's value, what defines a reliable stock options trading methodology, and your trading psychology.

Once thought to be the primary domain of highly qualified, skilled investors and traders, more private investors and traders enter the market for options today. Trading options can become the primary source of income for those who have the right education and mindset.

Several exciting and profitable alternatives to regular share trading are offered by options trading. But it is critical to be aware of the basic concepts involved before jumping in and getting involved in the trading of options. Options differ from stocks in that they are derivatives, meaning that options get their value from something other than themselves, i.e., an underlying security/share. There is also a time limit for options, while stocks do not. Options will expire after an agreed time, unlike inventories that do not, of course.

For some reason, people trade options. Firstly, they're an item capable of leverage. From minimal outlay, they can provide an excellent return. Of course, a double-edged sword is a leverage. If you win, you can do very well. Of course, if you lose, your losses are also magnified. Secondly, you can make money using different options strategies regardless of the direction of the market. If using technical analysis, charts, and indicators, you can accurately analyze a share's path. Then there is an options trading strategy that you can use to make money.

Their flexibility is another primary reason for engaging in options trading. By this, I mean you can trade in a sideways market or one that goes up (Bull market) or one that goes down (Bear market) and still makes consistent profits. You will need to be proficient with several vital skills and attributes to maximize your options trading success. They are abilities found in all successful traders of options.

1. an emotionally objective mindset

2. A solid understanding of the different strategies available to you

3. Find out which approach works best for you.

4. Good skills in technical analysis, such as charts, the use of indicators, etc.

5. A sound trading plan or system of investment

6. Discipline for trading

There is a risk involved, especially for beginners, as with any type of trade, and it is essential to seek the right education before you get involved. Of course, for just about everything in life, this is true. Once you have a strong foundation of education, you can build on it, always seeking to enhance your knowledge and refine your abilities and strategies. You will go a long way to minimize risk and maximize reward.

Before you invest a cent in the markets, invest first in your training in trading options. Finding a company with a range of courses to suit your needs, whether it is a beginner or an advanced trader, a company with professional instructors who all have years of trading experience, is the most efficient way to acquire your trade education options.

Selecting A Good Broker

It is paramount to your trade success to select the right broker to trade with. One of the keys to your trading company's success is a good broker known for fast and accurate executions of trades with all the tools and features required to trade in the current environment.

When comparing brokers to one another, one of the first things you want to look for is whether they specialize in the securities or investment vehicles you wish to trade. For instance, you're interested in Forex trading, short for foreign exchange markets. Don't pick a broker that is not a Forex specialist. Find a broker that offers Forex capabilities and tools primarily (or even exclusively).

With that same philosophy, you'll want to find a broker specializing in options if you're interested in trading stock options or index options. There is a specialist for every investment product and market out there, and there is no single universal" market to trade. So, you want to find a broker in your market that is experienced, professional, and reputable. The majority of brokers just can't be everything for everybody.

Ensure that the trades are simple to put on.

Since 99% of all trading nowadays is done via an Internet-connected computer, you want to make sure that your broker's trade execution software is easy for you to use. Consider using the "10-minute rule" if you're trying to compare the various trading platforms to and from each other. This rule states that if you cannot figure out how to place a trade within 10 minutes while logging in and browsing a broker's web-based software, the software is probably too complicated or too challenging to use effectively.

Also, look for brokers who have videos and instructions on using their platform and trading software. You don't want to spend time reading a manual and looking at screenshots of how to use the program; you want to learn through online videos in a convenient and accessible way.

Some software platforms are excellent but not incredibly intuitive or user-friendly, so you'll spend a lot of time and effort trying to maneuver around and understand all the features if you're going about it alone. However, if the broker has a good video walkthrough to show you step-by-step how to use their software, then you will have the best of both worlds: a strong understanding of the complex features offered by brokers that can enhance your trading skills and acumen.

Are the declarations of the account easy to read?

What do account statements for the broker look like? You'll want to be able to read and understand your broker's account statements easily so that you know where you are at all times. They must offer daily, updated online reports and metrics.

How long does it take to reach a person who is alive?

Reaching a live person on the customer service line is invaluable in so many different cases. For example, there may be times when you thought you had placed a trade in a certain way, only to find out later that you made a crucial mistake in your execution. You'll need to get a hold of a live representative in this and many other instances that can assist you right away.

When searching for the right broker that will allow you to execute profitable trades quickly and efficiently, take all these different tips and guidelines into account.

Develop A Trading Plan

The existence of a good trading plan is the crucial component of any effective trading. The obvious question for a beginner investing in the stock market is: what is a trading plan, and how do I create a good one? A process for evaluating stocks, identifying risk and profit goals, and planning a long-term investment strategy would define a trading plan. Moreover, determining a trading system such as Japanese Candlesticks will also include a good trading plan.

While realizing that even the best trading plan is not perfect, most successful traders maintain that the discipline of following their plan contributed to their success more than their investment philosophy. We understand that the evidence of a good plan is its results.

Trading tools, specifically technical analysis tools, are an addition to the success of a trading plan. When you integrate technical analysis with a candlestick chart analysis system, you can be assured that the components necessary to establish profitability in the market are included in your trading plan.

An investor must still understand and recognize when they have made investing errors and be able to recover with all of this power available. If a specific investment goes wrong, a good trading plan will include stop-loss strategies and techniques that allow an investor to have a pre-prepared plan. The difference between success in the general market and complete failure can be the preparation for such a situation.

Portfolio diversification is another significant concept in a trading plan. An excellent way to insulate an investment can be a portfolio with a wide variety of investment options, varying levels of risk, and diverse profit potential. This way, stock can be speculated on, and the rest of the portfolio can be used as a hedge against a devastating loss.

In a trading plan, what part does the investor play? The investor is the centerpiece of all successful or unsuccessful trade plan and the most important part! With euphoria, boredom, joy, pain, greed, and fear, all trying to shake an investor away from following their trading plan, the market is as much a mental adventure as anything. A trader who can withstand the market's emotions and adhere to the trading plan will have the best chance of success. Emotional reactions when investing almost always lead to bad decisions, as with most things in life. To avoid potential problems, avoiding investing in unknown markets, and resisting the temptation to start investing in the stock market because of boredom or peer pressure are suitable lessons to learn.

Investing certainly indeed has its share of pitfalls, and a good stock trading plan goes a long way to helping any investor who wants to enjoy profitable market trading. It is critical to take your time to develop a trading plan when starting to invest in the stock market, to acquire the necessary tools to assess businesses and their financial situations correctly, and to take advantage of learning from people who have gone through it all before. Although the market can be unpredictable, the principles and techniques needed to be effective have been used and have been shown to be quite reliable for years. A well-thought-out plan will provide the best investment advice an investor can ever receive and others' lessons.

Why Every Trader Needs to Develop A Trading Plan

You transport yourself to the world of global markets each time you fire up the trading software. You're going to travel! Your purpose for traveling to this world... is profit; your short-term goal is to return home with a profit. You are likely to search for capital growth, stability, income, and longevity in the long term. Experienced travelers use travel plans to go from one location to another, and for the stock market traveler, we strongly recommend trade plans.

The alternative is the attraction of risk. The short-term objective of profit is directly threatened by travel risk, but more importantly, it attacks your long-term goals of capital growth and longevity. The chances are the same, whether traveling to an unfamiliar city or the global stock market through trading. The risk is in the form of losing, wasting time, mismanagement of capital and strained decision-making, confusion, late to the party, unnecessary surprise, fear, and even running short of funds before the end of the trip. The risks are many, and the list goes on, but the point is: Effective trade plans inherently recognize and prepare you for the dangers of trading.

We don't merely travel down the street to our local food market when we trade (a short jaunt we can make with eyes closed). Hey, no. More precisely, we travel to foreign countries as traders... trips that require maps, research, preparation, and scheduling. This fact is why keen stock traders develop trade plans. Trade plans offer us all the benefits of a travel plan. Think of yourself as a traveler in the global market.

Trade plans are how we become effective traders, seen in their most encompassing light... they define our ownership of intent to succeed. Your macro or master trade plan creates a basis and future goal by answering large-scale questions: where do I start (departure), where do I go (destination), and how do I get there? (your chosen route).

How we make the least risk and safest return on each journey or individual trade is seen in their most concentrated light, micro, or daily trade plans. We answer questions smaller in scope at this level but no less important than those above: what indicators I use, how much I buy, what loss I accept, what profit is enough, etc.

You will develop your unique trade plan philosophy between the master trade plan and the daily trade plan; you will build a foundation, access, and make the best use of your experience and resources, developing organization, repeatability, and documentation. Trade plans are becoming a valuable training tool rather than just a useful trading instrument. In essence, business plans allow you to learn, grow, adapt, develop a pattern and routine, and eventually prepare you for the day you get lost. It may occur in a particular trade and last only a few hours, or three years into your global market travels and last for months. But we all experience the feeling of 'lost' at some point. Trade plans give us the ability to react to this emotional reality to promote our goals for growth and trade.

Does it sound complex, time-consuming, or overwhelming? It isn't. More naturally than one would think, trade plans present themselves. Remember, all we're talking about here is a travel plan being developed! For instance:

How do I get to my business conference from my house: how much is it going to cost, will I drive or fly, what am I going to pack, who am I going to know? What city am I going to be in, what is the weather like, what comforts do I need? Translate these questions into the terminology of trading, and you have: how do I get from my computer to a stock that I want to buy, how much it will cost, will I buy 200 or 2000 shares, what tools will I need, and what indicators will I use will I trade alone or with a group. Who do I know? What stock exchange do I trade, is the current sunny or cloudy feeling of the market, what aspects of trading are I most comfortable with, and what comforts do I need?

See you? When venturing into the global market, we want more than simple strategies; strategies alone will not produce self-sufficiency. Yes, we can charter a bus (find a stock picker) and allow this person to shuttle us on a pre-packaged sightseeing tour. Once in a while, this can be fun; this strategy even benefits. But it's not free of charge. And what happens on the day that we go to bed and miss the bus? We have paid in full already, and now we are left standing outside the motel holding the bag: lost. Well, if you've been reading with interest, you've already started the process of researching, developing your business plan, and building the foundation of self-sufficiency; you're not planning these trips for fun—but first for-profit, and then for capital growth.

Let's start the first leg of this trip together with a discussion of what will become a cornerstone of your trade plan's development, maps!

Since the beginning of time, maps have been a staple of human development, and the concept of maps in tandem with the development of a trading plan will serve you as a trader well. We mapped the stars, the continents, and the weather as people—cities, roads, and rivers. In reality, we have mapped history! The market world is so enormously large that it would be foolhardy to travel into their realm without a reliable set of maps. We use maps for direction, as a trader new to the profession. As a trader in the middle of our adventure, we use maps to navigate effectively and effectively. We use maps to plot the way back home as a trader nearing the end of our journey (daily or yearly).

Three key elements are provided by Maps: Scale, Compass, and Substance.

1. Maps provide scale: sites such as Google Maps operate so seamlessly, the concept of scale is easy to dismiss, but we see a brand new map with its unique limits every time we click 'zoom.'

Charting software and all facets of our trading research are subject to the same rules. When it comes to trading, choosing the correct scale—and zooming between multiple scales—is everything.

2. Maps provide a compass: studying a good map will lead us to ask the most appropriate questions and point us in a direction that promotes our journeys, research, and development of our trade plan. It is often tempting to see our "as-the-crow-flies." maps and trade plans. However, it is only the beginning to identify our starting point and our end goal—our entry and our exit. Between departure and destination, twists and turns of all magnitudes await us; we need a sound sense of compass to stay on course.

3. Maps offer substance: Each map tells us something different and valuable about where we are in a trade. For example, weather maps relate well to market sentiment—economic calendars, earnings, upgrades, and downgrades—information that impacts the climate of our area of interest. But even a great map will get us lost if we use it for the wrong purpose. Learning to evaluate the legend of each map is the key to knowing the substance.

Option Pricing Models

A magnificent "number crunching" trade tool is an option pricing model. Without it, the seat-of-our-pants are traded blindly. The difference between' knowing' and' guessing' is the difference. It'd be like a pilot flying without tools.

"It calculates implied volatility immediately, finds "best trade over/under assessments, finds "best.

Estimated results, both "on-the-fly" and at expiration, based on different scenarios,

And all those good things.

A model of option pricing gives us an "edge" against those who trade without one and another.

"levels the playing field" against those who do.

The market would close before if we had to do the calculations ourselves (good luck with that),

We're going to get something done.

But here is the thing: everything is theoretical! This fact isn't real. It's all work, of guess.

Forecasts are based on assumptions and guesses, which are nothing but educated guesses.

"It's very "iffy" stuff.

In forecasting, there is nothing wrong with using an option pricing model, per se, as long as it lasts.

We're never going to be right, as we realize. We will always be wrong. In an imperfect world, we strive for perfection. I'm so sorry I had to be the one to tell you.

All our advanced "toys" enable us to figure out what kind of guessers we are. To use an option pricing model, or any tool for that matter, is all good and good to

Before we commit to a position, try to pierce through the "fog" of the future.

Once we commit, though, it is no longer theoretical. It is ACTUAL!

From that point forward, price is the only thing that matters. Out the window is the theory. Have your goals, stop-loss points, and follow-up actions identified in advance and

Just stick with them. With that, too, a good option pricing model program can help us.

Manage the trade to its conclusion once a trade is established. Then proceed to the

Next trading. It is as straightforward as that.

CHAPTER TEN

RISK MANAGEMENT

The trading risk of options is defined as the likelihood of loss in trading capital. Option trading risks include the odds of losing your cash in layman's terms. Trading of options is not actual investing. Hoping to make a profit from market fluctuations is speculating and taking a calculated risk.

Become adept at predicting results to be a profitable trader. You also need to analyze circumstances and make trade decisions based on where you think the market will go - up or down. It can be a stressful decision, and it should not be made on the spur of the moment. If you are willing to take the risk, understand what you can lose, and only trade what you can afford to lose, trading options is precisely the practice of making money for you.

4 Points on Associated Risks to Ponder

Your objective is to make the odds move in your favor. This fact guarantees the success of your transactions. Do not be afraid to make mistakes and take risks; errors are where you learn how to earn rewards.

1. Create a strategy. There are highly volatile stocks, the commodity market, Forex, and indices. Options expire, and even on

investments, these types of trades win, lose or break. While you have the strategy to "play" the cash options you can afford to lose, remember that you are still using real cash and that losses can rise.

2. Options, since they are not long-term investments, are risky. Options are instruments that can provide leverage. Leverage works - win or lose - both ways. Make sure that you don't gamble all you have on a single trade. To maximize what you have to invest, spread out your transactions.

3. One danger is to believe that your underlying asset or choice is priced just right. You may over-speculate if you feel that options are "cheap," and if options are too high, you may only lose out on a winning chance. Watch the Volatility Index and CBOE NASDAQ Volatility Index of the Chicago Board Options Exchange to learn when to speculate and back off.

4. Trading options can be riskier if you don't have any expertise. In general, the less you know, the more you are going to lose, and using a demo account to minimize the losses and risk. This way helps you learn how to trade and what to do and reduces the number of mistakes you inevitably make. Read everything that you can and practice. To understand how to use the "real" trading platform, you can use demo trading platforms to explain what real-time trading looks like and provide a knowledge base.

By diversifying trades, minimize your risk. With binary options trading, this is very easy. You can choose from as many different asset classes and timeframes from brokers and platforms. You can hedge your winning edge by varying the underlying assets you trade-in and using multiple timeframe angles. When trading, practice smart money management methods. When you do not see a clear edge over the market, avoid risking your money. This strategy will help push the odds more in your favor with practice and record-keeping and minimize your risks.

Selling Options

Selling income options is one of those discourses widely embraced as a safe, conservative strategy recommended to their customers by retail brokerages when, in fact, consistently successfully selling options is a very complex trading strategy.

There was a time when Option Income Funds were all the rage, in a bygone era. Now, where are they?

Some studies have concluded that up to 80% of all options are worthless or, at least, not profitable for buyers. Really? The premiums paid must have been huge! If this was true, how did the Option revenue funds get blown away?

Understand one thing to begin with: Selling Options is a game where you win small and lose big. A lifetime of profits can be wiped out by one bad loss. That is not an overstatement. It has occurred, more than just on one occasion.

Traders of Successful Options are among the company's shrewdest, most advanced financial professionals.

It would be wonderful if writing an Option, waiting for it to expire worthlessly, and writing another Option were all that needed to be done when selling Options. You can even quit your job for the day. In dreams of yours!

Consider that with one call and one put-at-the-money plus at least one pair of each out-of-the-money and in-the-money, each new options series begins. That amounts to at least six new options available, two of which (33%) are in-the-money.

No matter what the entire market does (up, down, or sideways), it is guaranteed that at least two will end up in the money.

If the market moves up like a home-sick angel, the winners will be all the calls (three of the six). If the market crashes, all the Puts will be profitable (three of the six again).

Each strike price starts with four available expiration dates, and as the market passes through predetermined levels, new strikes are added.

All told, that's a lot to keep track of on anybody's plate. And this is only for one stock. How many constantly changing stocks do you want to monitor and their related options? The possible techniques used are practically unlimited. Good luck with that without a computer.

Traders with Professional Options are very much into math. Whether they buy, sell, or both (known as 'spreading'), the 'Greeks' are always aware of them (the theoretical mathematical components comprising Option pricing theory - see Black-Scholes Model, for instance. Try not to get a headache reading it).

Sellers of options (writers) make their money by selling an option's 'time value,' the out-of-the-money portion of an option's price (aka 'air' or 'puff'). If to start with, the option is out-of-the-money, the total cost consists of 'air' or 'puff' (some may call it 'hope'). The more 'heat' (volatility), the better the vendor wants to see the entire option expire worthlessly, quite naturally enough. Null. Zero. Oh. Zip. Huh. Nahda.

The seller (writer) will only have to come up with the stock to make 'delivery' if the option goes into-the-money (that is, having 'intrinsic value) if 'called' ('assigned' or 'exercised') in the case of a call, or in the case of a put, need to come up with the cash to buy the stock.

Sellers (writers) typically don't let it go that far if they can help it. Naturally, by buying back the options to 'close' their positions, they 'cover' their 'shorts.' They could even sell (write) another option called 'rolling' the place) and continue their campaign of trading options. The name of their game is to sell 'time value' and buy 'intrinsic value.'

Only a fool would sell uncovered options ('naked') (write). Why risk an unlimited loss as your only profit for a little credit? Professional traders prefer selling (writing)' spreads' for this reason.

'Spreading' means purchasing one option while selling another simultaneously. If the sold (written) option is higher in price than the purchased option, the position results in a net loan assumed with a known limited risk (distance between strikes less credit received).

Although the position has a lower potential profit due to the smaller credit, the trader can make the same dollar profit by increasing the number of spreads. For instance, if a 'naked' option takes 5 points with unlimited risk and a 'spread' takes 2 1/2 points with limited risk, it takes the same money to sell (writing) 2 spreads, and you sleep better.

Professional traders are always 'protecting' their positions. They must always be able to come back tomorrow no matter what happens today. Profits look after themselves. Losses never happen.

Forecast of Directions

It is not wrong to be concerned with the market's direction, but it is not a good strategy to trade stock options. Let us look at an example to understand this. Let's try and predict the winner of the NBL basketball game. If you had a favorite team, that's the team that didn't lose a match all season against a team that lost most of their matches all season, who would you choose to win the game? You would say, more than likely, the team that has won all season.

It's simple; all the facts, history, and analysis are there to predict who will win the match more than likely. This way is like trading directionally. You are concerned with the movement of a stock price in directional trading, that is, whether it goes up or whether it goes down. You win that trade if you have chosen the right one.

You need to keep in mind that it should not be about the direction of the price of stock options, but rather the size of the price movement of stock options when trading options or when trading stock options.

Let us once again look at that example. In the first instance, you need to pick a winning team no matter how much the team wins by even one point; a win is a win. What if the scores matter? What if the points were to be spread out? What if, to win the game, the favorite team had to win by a certain number of points? Things are starting to change a bit now. What if the favored team had 20 points to beat the other team?

This fact may not happen; sure, the favorites can win, but you have lost if they don't win by the point margin because the winning margin won't cover your cost.

Trading of options is precisely like the discussed example. You need to understand that you predict the size of the move if you are embarking on stock options trading.

The best part of this now, and that's why trading options or trading stock options is very lucrative, is that we can not only predict the size of the move, but we can also predict the likelihood of that move happening.

Market Trend

Almost all options traders have heard the age-old trading adage that says 'The Trend Is Your Friend.' Nonetheless, trading alternatives in the direction of the current market trend certainly puts the odds of winning in your favor. By purchasing call options in a bear trend market and buying put options in a bull trend market, too many beginners in options trading have lost entire accounts.

So what is a market trend exactly?

Trends on the market are like ocean tides. When you see the sea coming higher and higher up a beach, you know it's a rising tide, and you know it's a falling tide when you see more and more of the beach. Similarly, when you see the major indices like the Dow Jones Industrial Average or the S&P500 going higher and higher, you know it's a bullish trend. You know that when you see the major indices going lower and lower, it's a bearish trend.

Yes, market trends are general trends in which inventories appear to be moving. Most stocks' prices will move higher and higher in a bull trend, and the costs of most stocks will move lower and lower in a bear trend.

However, one thing to understand about trends is that trends are a "General Direction of Movement" This does not mean that the market only moves upwards every day in a bull trend, and it does not mean that the market only moves downwards in a bear trend.

If you observe ocean tides, the sea does not continue to rush to the beach in a rising tide but comes in "Waves," One wave above the previous one. The same thing is right of stock market trends. In a bull trend, you're going to see days up interspersed with days down. However, up days will happen more frequently and will make new highs after each slight retreat.

New traders who interpret the first down day in a bull trend as the market "turning bearish," this fact often comes as a surprise. This way is also how the proverbial "Bull Trap" and "Bear Trap" are short counter-trend moves that are misinterpreted as trend changes, fall for beginners and veteran options traders alike. As the general trend resumes and they are caught in a losing position that never gets turned around, traders who fall for either trap usually find themselves surprised.

Only the first step to recognizing market trends is to recognize how movements work. Have you ever conclude that the market is only to have a peer disagree with it in one direction? How can two people who look at the same market reach different conclusions about what the trend in the market is?

The complexity of understanding market trends comes with the realization that at any time, the market can indeed be in all three directions on the same day!

The market could be a bear trend for day traders, but it may be a bull trend for a swing trader on the same day and a neutral trend for a long-term investor on the same day. How would that be possible?

Depending on the time frame one trades on, there is not only one "Market" condition but countless market conditions! For different trading horizons and investment goals, the failure to recognize that market trend is different, leading to all the futile argument about what direction on TV the market is in.

If you have charting software, you may be shocked to see that often, depending on what time frame you are looking at, you will see a completely different chart pattern on the same index or stock; 1 min chart, daily chart, weekly chart, or monthly chart, each of them seems to tell you a different thing.

A chart that looks extremely bearish on the 1-min chart could look extremely healthy and bullish on a daily chart. As such, first and foremost, the analysis of trends requires an understanding of the exact time frame you are trading on.

It is an essential pre-requisite in options trading to recognize the exact time frame you are trading on where the options contracts and positions you purchased are time-sensitive! Yes, option positions do not last forever, and all options strategies have an ideal time frame within which an optimized return can be achieved.

For example, if you are trading day options and either writing or buying options to close them by the end of the trading day for a profit. The market trend you should be concerned with would be the intraday trend most commonly identified by the minute charts. In this case, your trading is no longer affected by whether the market is in a long-term bull or bear trend. The world might scream bullish, but if the minute charts are bearish for the day, then the direction from which you make your money is bearish.

If you are trading a Covered Call, if you intend to keep the stocks from being assigned, you might want to write the call options on a relatively sideways stock with the market trading within a range on the daily charts.

Conversely, if you buy long-term LEAPS options, you may be more concerned with the market's longer-term trend instead of being too worried about daily volatility.

So what are the most common instruments to use for recognition of market trends?

Many veterans can recognize the trend in a chart by merely looking at how the price chart looks. However, countless complex technical indicators have been invented over the less experienced or more technically inclined ages. Personally, the Simple Moving Average is the most time-tested, which is merely averaging the cost over some time to see where it usually moves towards.

CONCLUSION

Now it's time to step it up and enter the world of success in trading options. And you have to set up a bonafide trading objective to do so! More than just that. You need to come up with a specific monetary purpose.

Are you just investigating some fundamental knowledge of the trading of options? In options trading, are you new to getting started? If so, realize that there is a whole new world of opportunity for you out there. Start with a few hundred or a few thousand dollars, and you can make millions of dollars! And don't let any person ever tell you otherwise.

Remember that successful business people concentrate on what they want. They make goals and focus on the targets. Failures concentrate on the risks and focus on their fears and problems or potential future issues.

What is your intended purpose if you are involved in the online trading of options? Yes, that is a very significant point. To get involved in online options trading, you need to have a particular purpose. About why? Because you can get quickly distracted and off course in options trading, confused and lose focus of any original concept she had that inspired you to join options trading.

I have found from my experience that it is crucial to have a trading objective, a financial trading goal. In trading online options, it is important because having an economic purpose will help you bring everything together and acquire the knowledge and tools you need to succeed to get you to that goal. So, in other words, if you set sail at sea without a particular destination, unless you have unlimited fuel. You're going to be in trouble. The same goes for trading online options. And in trading online options, if you don't have an overall trading goal, you could either not make much money or lose money.

Once you have a trading objective, all you need is to master the book's strategies, and you will fly high in the trading world of options.

www.ingramcontent.com/pod-product-compliance
Lightning Source LLC
Chambersburg PA
CBHW070352220526
45467CB00001B/343